APOCALYPTIC PROBLEMS

APOCALYPTIC PROBLEMS

By the

Very Rev. H. ERSKINE HILL, M.A

Provost of St. Andrew's Cathedral, Aberdeen

Author of 'The Seven Parables of the Kingdom,' 'The
Parables of the Advent,' 'The Parables of
Redemption,' 'Manual of Faith
and Worship'

WIPF & STOCK · Eugene, Oregon

Wipf and Stock Publishers
199 W 8th Ave, Suite 3
Eugene, OR 97401

Apocalyptic Problems
By Hill, H. Erskine
Softcover ISBN-13: 978-1-7252-9107-2
Hardcover ISBN-13: 978-1-7252-9106-5
eBook ISBN-13: 978-1-7252-9108-9
Publication date 11/2/2020
Previously published by Hodder and Stoughton, 1916

This edition is a scanned facsimile of
the original edition published in 1916.

DEDICATED

to

M. E. H

PREFACE

SEVERAL of the chapters of this book have already appeared as articles in the *Expositor*. I have thought it best to leave them substantially as they originally stood, though this involves in one or two places a slight amount of repetition and overlapping. The last two chapters I have added because, though not dealing directly with the main subject, they illustrate the standpoint from which I have written.

I believe the Apocalypse to be a complete and intelligible whole embodying a progressive revelation deliberately given by our Lord through the agency of

angelic beings in a series of visions impressed on the inner consciousness of the
seer.   I am convinced that the purpose
of the book was to supply the Church with
the vision of the world and earthly life
as they see them, whose consciousness is
centred in the Spiritual and the Eternal,
and that only when this standpoint has
been attained will it be possible to put
to proper use the rich treasures which
scholarship supplies.   This volume only
claims to be a tentative effort to deal
with some of the problems of the Apocalypse from this point of view.   The
studies have been confined to the first
half of the book, while the short commentary, which I have tried to make as
simple as possible, only goes as far as
the eighth chapter.   I hope I may be
able in a later volume to complete the
commentary and to take up some more

of the many interesting problems contained in the latter part of the book.

My sincere thanks are due to my friend
and colleague, the Rev. P. M. Buchanan,
for kindly revising the proofs and for
furnishing me with several useful sug-
gestions.

St. Andrew's House,
    Aberdeen.

CONTENTS

Contents

Introduction

Introduction

THE Apocalypse was never intended
to be an obscure and cryptic
narration of concrete earthly events:
it is rather an unveiling of what earthly
events look like when seen from Heaven.
It deals with great principles, motives,
and tendencies which manifest themselves in human action. These it describes as they are seen by one who is
'in the Spirit.' It unveils the eternal
beauty which lies behind holiness, and
tears away the disguise from the monstrous form of sin. It is the priceless
gift to the Church of all ages of the
Angels' point of view. A series of wonderful visions are flashed on the inner
eye of the seer, and by them he is taught

as St. Peter was taught by the vision of
the Great Sheet at Joppa. The Angel
Guide uses the universal picture language
as the prophet-painter Watts uses it, but
the Angels' pictures are alive. We can
no more localize the Apocalyptic Babylon
than Bunyan's Vanity Fair or Doubting
Castle. We can no more identify the
Beast with an individual man than Watts'
'Mammon' or 'The Minotaur.' We
are in the realm of the abstract. The
message of the Apocalypse is age-long
and universal, applicable to every time
and place and wholly transcending both.
It gives the vision of the Infinite Wisdom, Love, and Power at the heart of
all things. It disperses for a moment
for the sin-darkened, sorrow-blinded
eyes of men, the clouds which are round
about Him, and shows that always and
everywhere the world is ruled from the
'Great White Throne.' It reveals the
power of self-sacrifice to solve the mystery of pain, and the power of the Living

Christ to give to His followers protection from all evil and victory over all temptation. It unveils the infinite resources of the might of Heaven and the limitations and ultimate overthrow of evil. It holds up to every man and to collective humanity a shining goal. It brings us in very truth, and as no other book does, to 'the City of the Living God, the heavenly Jerusalem and to innumerable hosts of Angels'—the bright company of spiritual helpers, and to those who have gone before us, 'the General Assembly and Church of the Firstborn.'

'Blessed is he that readeth, and they that hear the words of the prophecy and keep the things which are written therein.' Blessed is he who can see life and the things of life as they are seen from the Heaven side, and can frame his actions accordingly.

'*Felix qui potuit rerum cognoscere causas.*'

'The things which are seen are tem-

poral, but the things which are not seen
are eternal.' Yet the bodily senses
which bring us into touch with the
perishing world are alert and keen,
while the spiritual faculties which when
developed bring the eternal world round
us are often as unfolded as ' the wings
that sleep in the worm.' Thus for us
to-day, as for the distracted and persecuted Church of long ago, there is constant need for the unveiling of the unseen, and the Apocalypse is a living
book with a permanent message.

It may not be out of place here to
make a protest against the assumption,
to which some scholars who have dili-
gently studied Apocalyptic literature
seem peculiarly liable, that this book
is not really the record which it claims
to be of visions given to the writer when
' in the Spirit,' but rather a composition
in which he has deliberately borrowed
from previous writers not only the form
in which he has expressed his ideas, but

the ideas themselves, altering and adapt-
ing them to suit his own purpose in a
manner absolutely inconsistent with any
veracious record of a vision.   It is very
painful to find this assumption constantly
appearing in a writer so scholarly and
so reverent as Dr. Swete, in his really
great work on the Apocalypse. He
appears, for example, really to believe
that Isaiah had a vision in which he
heard the Seraphim cry, ' Holy, Holy,
Holy'; but when St. John describes
how he hears the same words spoken by
the Zoa, Dr. Swete's comment is ' Another loan from Isaiah's description of
the Seraphim. . . .   The Apocalyptist,
as usual, does not tie himself to his
source.' Is it quite inconceivable that
the words which ' they rest not day
and night, saying,' might be heard more
than once by human seers ?   Again, in
his note on the words of one of the Elders,
' The root of David prevailed to open
the book,' Dr. Swete remarks that ' the

Apocalyptist evidently finds satisfaction
in this title of Christ, *for he repeats it*
in xxii. 16,' where our Lord says to St.
John, ' I am the root and offspring of
David.' The assumption is clear that
in this latter passage St. John is not
really recording what was actually said
to him by Christ, but was putting into
His mouth a phrase which specially
appealed to himself. Again he says
that the vision of the four riders in chapter vi. has ' evidently been suggested
by Zechariah vi. 1,' but that ' the
Apocalyptist borrows only the symbol of
the horses and their colours, and instead
of yoking the horses to chariots he sets
on each of them a rider.' The one apparently impossible thing is that the Apocalyptist should ever see a vision for himself. In the same way Dr. Charles, in his
Studies in the Apocalypse, p. 113, when
discussing the four destroying winds,
says that ' we may reasonably conclude
that our author has made use of an

existing tradition to serve his purpose.'
We should probably feel less irritation
at remarks like these, if their authors,
instead of assuming, would condescend
to give some reasons for believing that
the Apocalypse is not what it professes
to be, a record of real visions, but only
a series of weird and composite word
pictures, largely borrowed and ingeni-
ously constructed like Bunyan's *Pilgrim's
Progress*, ' in the similitude of a dream.'

The Apocalyptic Element in our Lord's Teaching

I

The Apocalyptic Element in our Lord's Teaching

THERE has been in the last few years a remarkable concentration of attention by theologians and scholars on the subject of our Lord's Eschatological Teaching. This has become, in the words of the Dean of St. Paul's, 'The storm centre of Christian Apologetics.' A large field of study has been opened up. Current beliefs among the Jews with regard to the Messianic Coming, popular conceptions and misconceptions among the Early Christians about the Lord's Second Advent and the 'Day of Judgment,' and the so-called 'end of the world,' have all been carefully investigated.

Now there are several preliminary thoughts which we should do well to bear in mind in entering upon this study. First, let us realize the inadequacy of ordinary human language to deal with it. The Apocalyptic sayings of the Christ are an attempt to express in language which deals with things of sense and time, realities which transcend time and sense alike. Therefore, Apocalyptic sayings must of necessity be of the nature of hints, attempts rather to suggest than to portray, and the most suitable vehicle will be the parable. Hence also this kind of teaching will tend to acquire a technical vocabulary of its own and to have an esoteric meaning intelligible only to the few.

Perhaps the analogy may help us if we imagine a learned scientist trying to explain the mysteries of wireless telegraphy to some untutored aboriginal tribe. The teacher would be confronted with the double difficulty of the crudity of his hearers' minds and the extremely limited nature of their vocabulary.

Yet how trifling such difficulties would be, compared with the task which our Divine Lord set before Himself to translate into the language of time and sense, for the benefit of men to whom the phenomenal world alone seemed real, the great timeless spiritual truths of that eternal world in which His own consciousness was ever centred !

His sayings were constantly misinterpreted even by His Apostles, and He knew that they were misunderstood and left them unexplained. For He spoke for all ages. He left them as unintelligible as books are to babies, waiting until man should be sufficiently developed to understand them. There is something sublime in the calm certainty of His tone, and the assurance of His emphatic words—as though He anticipated the confused thinking of later ages, ' Heaven and earth shall pass away, but My words shall not pass away.' He spoke for all ages and His words can wait the development of the spiritual faculties by the aid of which alone they can be understood. From this point of view the popular opinions which prevailed in the primitive Church would seem to be comparatively unimportant as an aid to interpretation. Certainly they do not deserve the exaggerated importance which many scholars insist on assigning to them. Neither in that age nor in any age is it reasonable to insist that the sayings of those who know ' the mysteries of the Kingdom of Heaven ' are to be interpreted according to the intelligence of those to whom ' all these things are in parables.'

The sayings of the Christ round which many misconceptions rapidly gathered have been persistently interpreted in the light—if we can call it light—of these misconceptions, and many critics have read the popular belief in an immediate and spectacular Parousia into the words of the Master, until some ordinarily cautious and conservative writers have come to assume that the Christ Himself entertained an expectation that failed.

But if it is important to ascertain the standpoint of those to whom the words were spoken, it is surely far more necessary to make every effort to discover the standpoint of the Speaker, and this has not received the attention it deserves. Of course it is just here that mere scholarship fails us—or at least it must in this study take quite definitely a second place, and mystical insight must be our main guide. 'In this discussion,' says Principal Denney, 'the babes have the better of the philosophers.'

Let us pause for a moment on this

2

thought of the standpoint of the Speaker.
' I came out,' He says, ' from the
Father, and am come into the world.
Again, I leave the world and go unto
the Father.' There is movement then,
but no geographical movement—no
movement in the three dimensions we
know. God is no more ' above the
bright blue sky ' than beneath the deep
blue sea. Let us start from that great
saying of St. Bonaventura :

*' God, Who has His centre everywhere, and
His circumference nowhere.'*

The dense is always interpenetrated by
the less dense, and as we think of the
physical world interpenetrated by ether,
so we can think of ether as interpenetrated by still subtler media till we
come to pure spirit—to God who ' filleth '
—interpenetrates all.

' The God I know of I shall ne'er
Know though He dwell exceeding nigh.

Cleave thou the wood and I am there,
Raise thou the stone and there am I.
Yea, in my life His Spirit doth flow
Too near—too far—for me to *know*.'

If we can realize that as ether which
is the medium of the vibrations of light,
interpenetrates air, so it is interpenetrated by still finer forms of matter
which are the media of emotional waves
or waves of thought, then perhaps we
may think that the discussions of the
schoolmen as to the number of Angels
who could stand on the point of a needle
is not so insane as it sounds. There is
a real point in it.

And as we pass in thought from the
dense earth with its coarse vibrations
to the subtler vibrations of air, and ether,
emotion and thought—in and in till we
come to the central stillness—the conscious Bliss and Peace and Love which
is God—we have found a new dimension and a new direction. In the light
of that let us read again :

' I came out from the Father and am come into
the world.
Again I leave the world and go unto the Father.'
' He ascended that He might fill (interpenetrate)
all things,' and so come nearer to all.
' I go away and I come unto you.'   (R.V.)

' Ah, yes,' say nervous theologians,
' let us accept by all means the doctrine
of Immanence, but let us not forget to
balance it by the opposite doctrine of
Transcendence—otherwise we shall fall
into the errors of Pantheism and think
of God as limited by the universe which
He has made.'

Now if we put away the childish idea
that Transcendence means geographical
removal, we shall see that it is not an
opposing or balancing doctrine to the
doctrine of Immanence, but a continua-
tion of it.

We can only reach the true idea of
transcendence *through* Immanence and
—so to speak—out on the other side.

That is the idea contained in Chesterton's striking poem, ' The Holy of Holies ':

> ' Elder Father, though thine eyes
>   Shine with hoary mysteries,
> Canst thou tell what in the heart
>   Of a cowslip blossom lies ?
>
> Smaller than all lives that be,
>   Secret as the deepest sea,
> Stands a little house of seeds
>   Like an elfin's granary.
>
> Speller of the stones and weeds,
>   Skilled in Nature's crafts and creeds,
> Tell me what is in the heart
>   Of the smallest of the seeds ?
>
> God Almighty, and with Him
>   Cherubim and Seraphim,
> Filling all eternity—
>   Adonai Elohim ! '

' Filling all eternity.' What more can the most enthusiastic believer in Transcendence want than that ?

The less dense not only interpenetrates the dense, but transcends it.

It is never identified with it or limited by it.

Ether is present in every particle of matter, yet ether extends beyond the world and embraces the stars.

And so we can accept Faber's sayings :

' Out beyond the shining of the farthest star
  Thou art ever stretching—infinitely far ;
  Yet the hearts of children hold what world
    cannot,
  And the God of wonders loves the lowly spot.'
' God is never far enough away to be even near.'

Now starting from this thought we can see that there are two opposite standpoints from which we can look.

From the earth-side with the consciousness centred in the physical, we see first things or actions, then more remotely the feelings or emotions behind them, and farther off still the thoughts in which they originated. From the spiritual or Heaven-side, we should see in just the reverse order. The focus would be completely changed. Then the thought would be more visible than the feeling, and the action more remote than either.

If we grasp this I think we have the key to Apocalyptic teaching. Let me take an illustration from the fourth chapter of the Book of Revelation. From the earth standpoint the normal order of vision would be, first, the things of Nature, then the living forces behind them. Later on we should dimly reach the thought of great intelligent controlling powers, and finally arrive at the idea of God. But St. John is ' in the Spirit,' and he sees in exactly the reverse order. First he sees the Throne of God and Him Who sits thereon. Then the great Angelic Powers who rule the world for Him, the four and twenty Elders, then the living forces of nature symbolized by the four Living Creatures, and last of all the Creation itself—the ' sea of glass.'

Now let us return with this key in our hand to the account given in the synoptic Gospels of the discourse upon the Mount of Olives in answer to the question, 'When shall these things be and what shall be the sign of Thy Coming and of the Consummation of the Age ? ' In this connexion it is difficult to speak with patience of the culpable weakness of the revisers in allowing the monstrous mistranslation of συντελεία τοῦ αἰῶνος as ' the end of the world ' to remain in the text. It is not too much to say that the thought of Christians (including scholars) has been poisoned by the assumption that in this discourse our Lord is referring to the end of the world. Yet eminent scholars allow themselves to be led by the facility of a familiar and mistranslated phrase to assume that the Parousia involves the end of all things earthly. As a matter of fact the winding up of an age, the close of an epoch, which is all that the words imply, has no necessary connexion with ' the end of the world.' Ages have closed and civilizations been brought to an end again and again in the past, and the same process may be repeated again and again in the future. We shall never understand our Lord's Apocalyptic sayings till we cease to read them through the glare and haze of the *Dies Irae*, and learn to attach no more than their intrinsic value to the opinions of the σαρκικοί of the primitive Church, and to banish what we know is a mistranslation, if not out of the Bible, at least out of our minds.

There have been many ' great and terrible days of the Lord ' in the history of mankind, days of judgment in which the accumulated evil of the age at length bursts into flame and is burnt out in suffering ; ' benignant fever parox-ysms ' which pass and leave humanity prostrate but purified.

Such a day of judgment—not to go

far from our own times—was the French
Revolution, when the explosive material
to which every groan of the hungry and
oppressed under that gilded and corrupt
civilization had contributed at length
caught fire and smote the earth with a
curse.

> ' Down came the storm !   O'er France it passed
>   In sheets of scathing fire.
>   All Europe felt the fiery blast,
>   And shook as it rushed by her.
>
>   Down came the storm !   In ruins fell
>   The worn out world we knew,
>   It passed, that elemental swell,
>   Again appeared the blue.'

Such a ' great and terrible day of the
Lord ' at the time when the Christ
spoke His warning words was quickly
drawing nigh to bring to a close in
fire and blood the long age of Israel's
probation ; and its bitter obstinacy, its
stoning of the prophets, and all the
righteous blood that had been shed

while the age lasted was to be required of that generation.

Such a day of judgment on a far vaster scale we are passing through at the present time.

But all this has nothing to do with ' the end of the world.' It is among the pangs in which an old age perishes that a new age is born, and the world still goes on. ' *Et pur si muove*,' as Galileo said. Yet it is not without warning that epochs are so brought to a close. It was a matter of wonder to our Lord that even the Pharisees were unable to recognize the signs of the approaching doom. ' Ye know how to discern the face of the heaven,' He said, ' but ye cannot discern the signs of the times.' Nor is it necessary that progress should always be by overthrow, nor need these great days of the Lord always smite the earth with a curse. It is when an age is closing on a society rent by fissures deep and wide, when the hearts of rulers and ruled are estranged, when the hearts of the fathers are turned from the children and the hearts of the children from the fathers, that these days of visitation which might have witnessed an orderly and majestic evolution, bring instead a period of dreadful reckoning, of violence and destruction.

Perhaps this may seem too long a digression to hunt out one particular error, but I am convinced that so long as it dominates the situation, thinking on our Lord's apocalyptic teaching must remain hopelessly confused.

Let me give one or two examples of the way in which well-known thinkers have allowed themselves to be entangled by this error.

'So wise a man as the late Henry Sidgwick,' said Bishop Gore at a recent Church Congress, 'was alienated from the faith and membership of the Christian Church mainly by the conviction

that Jesus Christ had certainly proclaimed the immediate coming of the
end of the world, and that it had not
come as He prophesied. Jesus, he
thought, was certainly under a delusion,
and could not therefore be what Christendom believed Him to be."

Principal Denney speaks in very
guarded language, and yet his meaning
is not doubtful. 'When all qualifica-
tions are made,' he writes, ' it is impossible for any candid reader to get rid
of the fact that Jesus conceived the
triumph of the Kingdom to come with
His own Coming in glory, and that He
spoke of it as so near that the very
people whom He addressed must be in
constant readiness for it.'

And again, ' Jesus knew that the
powers of the world to come were present
in Him, and that the coming of the
Kingdom was sure. God would triumph,
and God's triumph would be His : He
had no doubt of that. But God's

triumph was not only sure ; to the spirit
of Jesus, Who laid down His life for it,
it was urgent ; it *could* not be delayed ;
adhuc enim modicum aliquantulum, yet
a little, ever so little, while, and He that
cometh shall come. Does it change our
attitude to Jesus to think of Him thus ?
Are we the less able, or the less willing,
to call Him Lord when we realize that
in the days of His flesh He walked by
faith, and that the assurance of His
triumph, and of God's triumph in Him
—in which all history is His justification
—did not enable Him to hold up to His
disciples a mirror in which the course
of history could be foreseen ? In substance His words are true, but as in all
prophecy the form is inadequate to the
substance ; and this state of the case
must simply be recognized.'

'The most important thing about
the Second Advent in the New Testament is that in its dated and spectacular
form it disappears. The last of our

gospels, which is ascribed not only by uniform Christian tradition, but by its own unequivocal testimony, to the disciple whom Jesus loved, has nothing to say of it. It was written when the Church had not only known, but, in this great spirit at least, outlived all its embarrassments about the delay of the advent. The eschatological hopes of the earlier gospels are not simply omitted in John : they are replaced. Instead of the apocalyptic discourses of Jesus, as at the close of Matthew and Mark, we have the intimate discourses of the upper room. Instead of a coming of the Son of Man on the clouds of heaven, we have the coming of the Spirit, the alter ego of Jesus, into the souls of believers. The evangelist takes it for granted that in this substitution of a spiritual for an outward coming he is true to the mind of the Master. He does indeed speak words which refer to the resurrection of Jesus, to His appear-

ing to His own, and to a final day of
judgment : but substantially the speedy
triumph of which Jesus spoke in Apocalyptic language resolved itself for Him
into the victory of the Spirit over the
world.'

He speaks of this as a ' bold transmu-
tation of the predictions of Jesus which
was forced on the evangelist by the
teaching of events and by the Spirit.'

Another well-known scholar seeks to
break out of the snare in another direction.

' Did Christ,' he asks, ' expect an
immediate Parousia ?   His disciples,
after His Ascension, did apparently
anticipate His speedy return, and they
were wrong. But did He not expect
that His Messianic vindication was near
at hand, even in the days of His public
ministry ? How are we to deal with
such passages as " Ye shall not have
gone through the cities of Israel, till
the Son of Man be come," and " There be

some of them that stand here which shall not taste of death till they see the Son of Man coming in His Kingdom ? " I will say quite frankly that if we had no report of the Lord's words but that in St. Matthew there would be no escape from the conclusion that in these sayings He anticipated a manifestation of the Son of Man, which, in fact, did not take place. There was no such manifestation before the disciples returned from their mission, nor did any of them see the Son of Man coming with power. But no principle of Synoptic criticism is better established than this, that Matthew is a secondary authority as compared with Mark. When the same thing is reported by both, Mark is the original source which Matthew has edited. Now take the last quoted saying as it appears in Mark—" There be some here which shall not taste of death till they see the Kingdom of God come with power." There is not a word about the Son of Man ; it

3

is the coming of the Kingdom that is
spoken of, and he would be a bold inter-
preter who would deny that this was
fulfilled at Pentecost. Or, again, ex-
amine the context in Matthew of the
saying about the disciples going through
the cities of Israel. It follows a prediction of tribulations. Where does that
prediction appear in Mark ? Not at
all in reference to the mission of the
Twelve, but in the Apocalyptic discourse
spoken before the Passion. Whatever
the original form of St. Matthew x. 23
may have been, it was not spoken, unless
Synoptic criticism is wholly at fault, in
connexion with the preliminary excur-
sion of the Apostles. I do not know
a more striking illustration of the gains
that New Testament criticism has
brought to us than is suggested here.
An examination of the internal rela-
tions between St. Matthew and St. Mark
disposes of the perplexity which such
sayings of Christ as those just quoted

present in their Matthæan context. When reference is made to St. Mark there is seen to be no ground whatever for the suggestion that they imply an expectation on the part of Christ of a glorious manifestation of Himself in judgment in the immediate or the near future. The Apocalyptic discourse of St. Mark xiii., in which the Fall of Jerusalem and the end of all things are both discussed, presents a difficulty which cannot be thus explained, as every reader of the Gospel knows. I must leave it for discussion by those who follow me, and I will only say this about it—the report of this discourse is obviously so much abbreviated that there can be no question of verbal precision in the record ; and hence the exact context of the words, " This generation shall not pass away until all these things be accomplished," cannot be certainly established.'

Once again so careful a scholar as

Dr. Swete commenting on the words from Revelation, about ' the trial which is coming on the whole habitable earth,' writes : ' i.e., the troublous times which precede the Parousia. In the foreshortened view of the future which was taken by the Apostolic Age this final sifting of mankind was near at hand, not being yet clearly differentiated from the imperial persecution which had already begun.' Now what authority has Dr. Swete for reading ' final ' into the prophecy ? Why should he assume that a ' coming ' of the Christ necessarily implies ' the end of the world ? ' It is the old error lying at the back of all these wrestlings with the text—the habit of assuming that our Lord meant His sayings to be interpreted by the not very enlightened minds of the first Christian communities ; as if we had any right to expect that they were entirely free from those persistent tendencies to secularize spiritual sayings for which our Lord was continually rebuking His Apostles.

I would humbly suggest that regarded apart from this distorting medium there is not one word which justifies us in thinking that either the Christ or those Apostles who heard Him, believed in His immediate visible return to the world after His Ascension. If St. Paul in his earlier writings appears to share the popular belief, yet in his later epistles a truer perspective is apparent.

Let me take an example of the way in which sayings seem to me to have been altogether misapplied.

There are no words which have been more generally taken to refer to the Second Coming of our Lord than those in the first chapter of the Apocalypse.

' Behold, He cometh with clouds and every eye shall see Him and they also that pierced Him and all kindreds of the earth shall wail because of Him. Even so. Amen.'

Yet I think if we can break away from

the traditional attitude, we may see that St. John in these words is looking back on the first Advent ; for he is quoting musingly two passages from the Old Testament, blending and applying them, repeating them in view of his own experience.

'Behold, He cometh with clouds,' so says Daniel, 'and every eye shall see Him.'

'They shall look on Me,' says Zechariah, 'whom they pierced.' How true ! How wonderfully it has all been fulfilled. Yes—every eye shall see Him and they also that pierced Him—

'With clouds,' *veiled,* that is, *from worldly sight.* The writer of Daniel, and St. John after him, are using technical Apocalyptic language. 'With clouds' ; how wonderfully applicable to His First Coming !

We can think of the clouds as rent indeed for a moment to the eyes of the shepherds of Bethlehem—rent for a moment when the star shows through that 'led on the grey-haired wisdom of the East,' but at Nazareth they closed over Him again. So as He begins His Ministry, men ask, 'Is not this the carpenter?' He comes with clouds. So it was designed—He does mighty works, yet He says, 'See thou tell no man'— 'He straitly charged them that they should not make Him known.' The Pharisees demand a coming 'with observation.' They want a sign from heaven and He sighs deeply and leaves them. He draws the veiling clouds round Him. He will not disperse them, nor suffer them to be dispersed. Shortly before His Crucifixion, He lays upon His future preachers the solemn charge that they should 'tell no man that He was the Christ.'

'Behold, He cometh'—He ever cometh —not 'with observation,' but 'with clouds.' Physical eyesight cannot pierce them, clever intellect cannot pierce them, but intuition, faith, spiritual vision can.

We think of another scene when the Master asks His disciples, ' Who do men say that the Son of Man is ? ' and St. Peter answers, ' Thou art the Christ, the Son of the Living God,' and we notice the joy with which He welcomes this evidence of the faculty of mystical insight in His follower. ' Blessed art thou, Simon Bar-Jonah, for flesh and blood hath not revealed it unto thee '—the clouds are still there, but faith has pierced them. ' Now I can begin to build My Church. Your answer,' He seems to say, ' shows the development of a faculty in that part of your being which is beyond the reach of Death.'

So we understand the deep Ναί, ἀμήν of St. John as he musingly dwells on the words of the prophets with his eyes on his own memories of the Incarnate Life.

' Behold, He cometh with clouds, and every eye shall see Him and they also that pierced Him and all kindreds of

the earth shall wail because of Him.
Even so. Amen.' He sees the deep
penitence all down the ages as the meaning of the eternal sacrifice dawns on
generation after generation.

Similarly, let us take those words, which
we have just seen thrown overboard to
lighten the ship, in which our Lord
tells His disciples that ere that generation had passed away they should see
' the Son of Man coming in a cloud with
power and great glory.'

These words also have strangely been
taken to refer to the Second Coming,
but surely that is a mistake. ' What
shall be the sign of Thy Coming ? ' they
had asked. We know that when they
asked it, they did not for a moment
expect the great eclipse of Calvary, to
be followed by the Resurrection and
Ascension. They believed and rightly
that the age was near its close and that
their Master was to be ' manifested to
the world.' But they altogether mis-

understood the manner in which He would reveal Himself. 'By Thy Coming,' they clearly meant 'Thy manifestation.' [1] They were far indeed from thinking then of a *Second* Coming.

In this same sense we understand our Lord's saying, 'Ye shall not have gone over the cities of Israel till the Son of Man be come.' So in answer to their question which, as we have seen, had nothing whatever to do with a Second Advent, our Lord replies in the traditional language of Messianic prophecy and tells them that ere that generation passed away, they should 'see the Son of Man coming in clouds with power and great glory.'

Notice how different the meaning of these words is when interpreted from

[1] Cf. the tone of dismay in the question, 'Lord, what is come to pass that Thou wilt manifest Thyself unto *us* and not unto the world?' (St. John xiv. 22).

the standpoint of Earth and from the standpoint of Heaven.

By ' clouds ' does our Lord mean a congregation of vapours or does He use the word as the symbol of that which veils ?

By ' Power ' is He referring to power like that wielded by Pontius Pilate— ' power to crucify ' or to the power of the pierced Hands—the power to be crucified ?

' He had rays coming out of His Hands, and there was the hiding of His power.'

And what is glory ? Is it the tinsel flash of earthly splendour ? Or is it manifestation of the going forth of Love ?

' And now, O Father, glorify Thou Me with the glory that I had with Thee before the world was.' That is, ' Let the going forth of Thy love be made manifest through this mortal Body.' And the answer to that prayer was the Crucifixion.

Tu Rex gloriae, Christe.

St. John the Baptist's conception of the First Coming is extraordinarily like the popular conception of the Second which prevails to-day. He accepted the traditional belief. He identified Jesus with the Messiah, and he watched and waited and expected. When would He ' come ' ? When would He appear in clouds of light and splendour ? When would He assume His power and manifest His glory ?

In his prison we can imagine how he eagerly questioned his disciples as to the attitude of the authorities and of the populace—What is He doing ? ' Going from place to place,' they tell him, ' teaching, healing, casting out demons.' ' Then is the Messiah,' he thinks, ' a still later comer ? Are the clouds and the power and the glory to belong to another and is Jesus just carrying on my work of preparation ? ' So he sends his message, ' Art Thou he that

cometh or look we for another ? ' (note
the use of the word ' cometh '). And
the men deliver their message and then,
like orientals, wait while the Master
teaches and heals.

Then His answer in effect is this,
' Do not clouds surround Me ? Is not
power going forth from Me and manifested love ? Is not the sign of My true
Kingship the number whom I can help
and serve ? The world does not understand this, but the spiritually minded
will see, and blessed is he who shall
not be offended in Me.'

We can imagine the effect on St. John.
It is ' not with observation ' then !
Silently—unrealized—the Coming will
soon have taken place ! So He came
in a cloud with power and great glory
—so when their eyes were opened His
followers saw, and ere the nation realized
it was judged. We look forward to a
Second Coming of our Lord. What
are our conceptions of ' clouds ' and

' power ' and ' glory ' ?   Have we not like
the Jews, and like the Baptist, and the
Disciples, materialized them ?   Have
we not as they did surrounded the
thought of the Coming with all kinds of
crude, material interpretations of spiritual figures till—if He should appear to
His world, as He did 1900 years ago
to the Jewish nation, unbelief would
be demanding the expected visible ' signs
from Heaven,' and worldliness and preju-
dice would be as blind as then, and the
world like Israel long ago would be
judged ere it knew.

' Tell us, when shall these things be
(the overthrow of the Temple) and what
shall be the sign of Thy Coming and of
the Consummation of the Age ? '

It was a comprehensive question and
our Lord's reply looks as if it might be
divided into three distinct parts.   He
gives first in general terms the signs by
which the close of an age may be recognized.   Then He gives His followers

the immediate signs of the closing of
that particular age, and finally He
answers the question as to the signs of
His own Coming (not His Second Coming, let us note ; they had no thought
of that—but of His manifestation).

Generally the signs which herald and
accompany the close of an age are excite-
ment and tumult, wars and rumours of
wars, earthquakes, famines, and a widespread turbulence, which seem to indi-
cate that some restraining power is
being withdrawn.

When an age—or civilization, as we
call it—is beginning, progress is slow,
century after century passes with little
change, and precedent is slowly added
to precedent ; but toward the close
things begin to move with ever-increas-
ing rapidity. Men feel themselves borne
along helplessly by forces and tendencies
which they cannot control, and toward
issues which they can only dimly and
fearfully descry. Our Lord sums up

the experience in one graphic and suggestive phrase, 'These things are the
beginning of travail,' the birth-pangs,
that is, of the age that is to be.

Then naturally and inevitably He
goes on to deal with the events which
would precede and accompany the close
of that particular age and of what we
call the Jewish Dispensation. Accordingly He warns His followers when they
see Jerusalem compassed about with
armies to flee to the mountains, and
specially He puts them on their guard
against pretenders who in that time of
fearful crisis should claim to be the
Christ. In St. Matthew's account, a
significant hint is added to this warning.
They need not fear that there is danger
to them of failing to recognize His Coming. To them there will be no possi-
bility of mistake. 'For as the lightning cometh forth from the East and
shineth even to the West, so shall the
Coming of the Son of Man be.' His Call,

that is, will be unmistakable to His own ;
whenever He may come, wherever they
may be, they will hear and recognize
His voice, but the world will not see
that which is to them as plain and all-
pervading as the lightning flash, and
so He adds, ' Wheresoever the carcase
is thither will the eagles be gathered
together.' It is amazing that a theo-
logian like Chrysostom should so entirely
miss the meaning of these words as to
see in them a reference to the Eucharist,
and hardly less astonishing that some
more modern commentators have fancied
there was some reference to the eagles
upon the Roman Standards ! Surely
the point of the hint is the keenness
of the vultures' sight. A camel falls
in the desert and straightway from
North and South and East and West the
vultures, till then hidden in the far-off
blue of the sky, hasten to the prey, which
they and they alone among the creatures have seen. They have eyes to

4

see what to the rest is invisible. Even so His Coming, unrecognized by the world, is visible to all who spiritually have eyes to see. And what are we to make of the concluding part of the discourse which speaks of the darkening of the sun and moon and the falling of the stars and the Vision of the Son of Man and the gathering of His elect. All is to take place ' after that tribulation ' (i.e., the destruction of Jerusalem) and before that generation should pass away.

I would suggest that not only this limitation of time but the nature of the words themselves would lead us to interpret them as referring, not to some future cataclysm in history but to a transcendental experience, which was literally fulfilled in the lifetime of some at least of those who heard them. Under the Master's training their spiritual faculties had been awakened and were rapidly developing, and the spiritual

world was ready to burst upon their
inner vision, just as the world of colour
waits to grow round the blind man whose
eyes are being opened. Flashes of revelation, glimpses of truth, visions of
spiritual realities begin to break in upon
the awakening inner sight, showing that
' He is nigh—at the doors.' The consciousness of the seer, hitherto centred
in the phenomenal, begins to transcend
it and to centre itself in the timeless
and eternal, and the change is like wit-
nessing the break-up of the world. To
one whose inner eye is opened to the
glow of ' the light that never was by
sea or land,' all that has before seemed
brightest—the sun that was the very
symbol of brightness—grows dark by
comparison ; and compared with the
glories of that eternal world the stars
themselves—those shining, age-long symbols of permanence—are like so many
autumn leaves cast from a tree. ' The
sun shall be darkened, and the moon

shall not give her light and the stars shall be falling from heaven.'

And then to the awakening spiritual sense there becomes visible the great continuous Coming of the Son of Man —the vision of 'the Light that lighteth every man' coming like a great dawn into the world. The age-long truth is manifested of which the First Advent, as we call it, is but a reflexion under conditions of time and space, and along with this there is seen when viewed from the Heaven side the gathering together into one mighty host of God's elect who seem to earthly eyes so feeble and scattered and isolated. The nature of the vision is inevitable when we realize the change of standpoint.

'And then shall they see the Son of Man coming in clouds with power and great glory; and then shall He send forth the angels and shall gather together His Elect from the four winds, from the uttermost part of the earth to the uttermost part of the heaven.'

What is the First Coming of
Christ ?

II

What is the First Coming of Christ ?

IT is generally assumed that 'The First Coming' of Christ dates from His Birth in Bethlehem, and that His frequent references to the 'Coming of the Son of Man' are to be applied to His 'Second Coming.' There can be no question that He spoke of that Coming as close at hand, in the lifetime of some of His hearers. 'Ye shall not,' He says, 'have gone over the cities of Israel till the Son of Man be come.' It is generally assumed again that the promise so clearly made remains to this day unfulfilled. The more reverent critics question the

55

accuracy of the Text and the less reverent impute mistake to the Christ Himself. It is a mild expression of the truth to say that Christian thought on the subject is seriously distracted and confused. I am profoundly convinced that both the assumptions referred to above are entirely false, that the First Coming of Christ to the world had not taken place when He spoke of the impending Coming of the Son of Man, and that the Coming did take place in the lifetime of some who heard the promise made. When we speak of the Christ as ' coming to the world' at Bethlehem, we are using a phrase which is ambiguous and confusing. It is true in one sense, and untrue in another. He took human nature upon Him then, ' He was in the world,' He entered earth-life, He was made man. In that sense He may be said to have ' come to the world.' But in the larger sense of His Coming as Son of Man to the world of men, it was still an event of the future. It did not take place, and it could not have taken place, till after the Crucifixion. In the Body which He took of the Virgin Mary, and in which He was crucified, He came as the long-promised Messiah to the Jews. He was born under the separating restrictions of the Jewish Law. His mission in the flesh was strictly limited. He was ' not sent but to the lost sheep of the house of Israel.' ' He came unto His own possessions, and they that were His own received Him not.' His Divine love longed to overflow the limits of His commission. ' I have a baptism to be baptized with,' He cried, ' and how am I straitened till it be accomplished ! ' The request of the Greeks at the Feast, ' Sir, we would see Jesus,' brought upon Him, when He heard it, the pangs of the Crucifixion. He realized in that hour that only by His death as a Jew could He free Himself from the restrictions of the Jewish Law and reach the world and become the Saviour of the world. That is the thought behind the words, ' Verily, verily I say unto you, except a grain of wheat fall into the ground and die it abideth alone, but if it die it bringeth forth much fruit,' and again, ' I, if I be lifted up from the earth, will draw all men unto myself.' It was to the Jews that He came in His physical Body, and in it He found His infinite love hedged in by legal and lifelong restrictions and His energies circumscribed. His Death alone would break down the separating barriers and rend the veil and bring Him into saving contact with all. So by His Crucifixion He ' blotted out the bond written in ordinances that was against us (Gentiles), which was contrary to us and,' in the magnificent rhetoric of St. Paul, ' took it out of the way, nailing it to the Cross.'

For His Coming to the world He needed a Body which could be diffused throughout the world and which could live from age to age. It was in His Mystical Body and on the Day of Pentecost that His First Coming as Son of Man to the world took place. Just as He became incarnate by the Holy Ghost of the Virgin Mary and took from her the Body in which He performed His earthly ministry, so on Pentecost He became incarnate by the Holy Ghost in His Body the Church. It is altogether a mistake to speak or think of the Holy Ghost as a substitute for an absent Christ. He is, on the contrary, the Medium of Christ's Presence. Now, if His First Coming to the world as Son of Man took place at Pentecost, we get rid at once of all the difficulties which have troubled those who assumed that His First Coming took place at Bethlehem and that it was to His Second Coming that He referred when He said, ' Ye shall not have gone through the cities of Israel till the Son of Man be come.' When the disciples asked, ' What shall be the sign of Thy Coming,' they clearly spoke of a First, not of a Second Advent. We have assumed that they considered that their Master had ' come ' already, that they knew of His approaching separation from them, and that they asked when they might expect Him again after the separation was past. It seems quite plain that we have read into their words a meaning which simply could not have been theirs.

In removing this difficulty by showing that many of the allusions to the Coming of the Son of Man refer to the First and not to the Second Advent, it must not be thought that we are throwing any doubt on the latter. At the very time of His withdrawal at the Ascension the promise was made which can only refer to a Second Coming, ' This same Jesus whom ye have seen taken into Heaven shall so come in like manner as ye have seen Him go into

Heaven.' That is quite plain and definite as a promise, and it does not stand alone. Nevertheless, I feel sure that many of the popular ideas as to the manner of His promised Second Coming would have been different in many respects had not the mystical language in which our Lord spoke of His First Coming been crudely and literally applied to His Advent which is yet to be.

The Mystical Significance of
Apocalyptic Numbers

III

The Mystical Significance of Apocalyptic Numbers

IT is quite possible to overdo the search for a mystical significance in numbers. A recent writer, for example, has pointed out that the number 153 referred to in St. John xxi. 11 is made up of $3 \times 3 \times 17$. I do not remember that the analysis carried us much further into the heart of the mystery, nor do I see more reason for analysing the number of fishes caught than the number of the cubits (about 200) which divided the ships from the land at that particular time. 200 is made up of $10 \times 10 \times 2$. What after all is more likely than that an aged fisherman, whose duty perhaps it had been to count the fish caught for purposes of sale, would vividly recall the precise number of a miraculous and record catch ?   On the other hand, it is quite impossible to study the Apocalypse without recognizing that numbers are constantly, and we might even say exclusively, used in a symbolical and mystical sense. There is a science of numbers and it is based on certain fundamental facts. Thus God has revealed Himself as Three in One, and it would seem that for this reason 3 becomes the number typical of Heaven. In the fourth chapter of this book, which opens with the Vision of the Supreme Throne and Him who sits thereon, we cannot fail to notice the striking fact that again and again we meet with triads, ' Lightnings and voices and thunders ' ; ' Holy, Holy, Holy, is the Lord God, The Almighty, which was, and which is, and which is to come ' ; ' Glory, and honour,

and thanks'; 'The glory, and the
honour, and the power'; as though
the threefold Majesty of God which
dominates the chapter threw its reflection on the very phrases in which heavenly things are described.

Again, 4 is taken as the typical
number of Earth. Animate creation is
represented by the four living creatures,
while men are spoken of as purchased
from 'every tribe, and tongue, and
people, and nation.' The first four of
the seven seals refer to the causes of
sufferings which afflict the world and
in which animate creation shares. The
hymn of praise offered by 'every created
thing' takes a fourfold form, 'The
blessing, and the honour, and the glory,
and the dominion.' The destructive
forces of the world are shown as the
four winds held in control by four
angels, standing at the four corners of
the earth. The Holy City Jerusalem
which is seen 'coming down out of

heaven from God' is revealed as combining the number of earth and the number of heaven. It has 4 sides, and each side has 3 gates. 'It lieth foursquare,' and 'the length and the breadth and the height thereof are equal.' Its characteristic number is 12 or 4 × 3. In short, we may say that from these two root numbers of 3 and 4 all, or almost all, the other mystical numbers of the Apocalypse are derived. Thus, earth and heaven in union give the number 7, which is treated as representing perfection, while blended into a permanent unity they give the number 12. When in the fifth chapter the angels join the four living creatures and the four and twenty elders, the hymn of praise, the ' New Song,' becomes sevenfold, ' Power, and wisdom, and riches, and might, and honour, and glory, and blessing ' ; while the great ascription of praise in chapter vii., in which men and angels join, is also sevenfold. Then

we have the seven Seals, the seven
Trumpets, and the seven Bowls, and in
each case the temporal effects are represented by the first four.[1]

What the Seven Thunders uttered
(ch. x. 4) the Seer was forbidden to
write.

That 7 is not arbitrarily fixed as the
number of perfection would seem to be
indicated by the fact that it takes 7
notes to complete the scale, and 7 colours
go to make up the ray of light, while
upon man, ' strange composite of earth
and Heaven,' the number seems to be
deeply impressed, so that in periods of
seven his physical development moves.
Again from the fact that 7 is the number
of perfection we obtain as representing

[1] It is not without interest that the Seven
Parables of the Kingdom as related in St. Matthew's
Gospel are similarly divided, the first four being
told to the multitude, and the remaining three,
which deal with deeper mysteries, are told after-
wards to the disciples alone.   St. Matthew xiii.
34–36.

that which falls short of it the number 6, which will be dealt with later. Perhaps it may be that because 13 similarly just falls short of the double 7 it is so persistently regarded as an 'unlucky' number. But let us consider a little further the number 12. There is much to lead one to think that there are 12 fundamental types of humanity, and that when God specially prepared a race with which to work out in history in a concrete and typical way a parable of the age-long deliverance of man from the bondage of materialism into the glorious liberty of spiritual freedom, it was organized in twelve tribes, each with strongly marked characteristics of its own, and on these characteristics emphasis in the inspired writings is repeatedly laid. (See Gen. xlix., Deut. xxxiii.) There does not seem to be any other satisfactory explanation of the amazing share which Hebrew literature and Hebrew history take in the

thought of the world. Why, it may be
asked, should the historic imagination
of men be so concentrated on the deliverance of this pigmy nation from Egypt,
its experience in the wilderness and its
entrance into Canaan ? Its own greatest
writers claim for its history a world-
wide, age-long significance. 'These
things,' says St. Paul, 'happened unto
them by way of figure' (τυπικῶς). It
may well be questioned whether the
full significance of these words has been
properly grasped. If, then, Israel was
chosen as a type of humanity, and if
its twelve tribes represent twelve fundamental and permanent types—and their
reproduction in the typical list of the
redeemed and in 'the Holy City, Jerusalem,' surely suggests this—then much
becomes intelligible which would otherwise be obscure. The organization of
Israel in twelve tribes, their symbolic
representation in the breastplate of
Aaron by twelve precious stones, the

choice of the twelve Apostles, the promise given to them by their Lord that
in the Palingenesis, or ' regeneration,'
they would ' sit on twelve thrones judg-
ing the twelve tribes of Israel ' all point
in the same direction. It is remarkable as showing that the choice of the
number 12 is neither arbitrary nor temporary, that while one of the original
tribes—that of Dan—fails and is omitted
from the list given in chapter vii. from
which the hundred and forty-four thousand are sealed, its place is taken by
the tribe of Manasseh in order that the
number may be complete. In a similar
way one of the original twelve Apostles
fails, and the failure is predicted as
though in some sense inevitable, ' that
the Scripture may be fulfilled,' but here
too it was felt to be necessary that the
vacant place should be filled by another.
Eleven tribes or eleven Apostles would
not represent a complete humanity.

Another problem is presented by the

four and twenty elders.   Who are they,
and why are they so numbered ?   A
first and very obvious step towards the
solution is to recognize that here again
the twelve types are still represented.
We are dealing with 12×2. It is
therefore the latter figure which demands
study.   We have to inquire why each
type should have a double representation.   Our answer to that will depend
on the explanation given of the identity
of the elders.   Who are these mighty
ones who ever acknowledge the sove-
reignty of the supreme throne, casting
their crowns before it, yet are themselves
Rulers enthroned and crowned, and who
moreover interpret and express the vast
worship of creation ?   They are differentiated from the Angels and are closely
associated with nature and with man.
The very name ' Elders ' seems to link
them to humanity, while the crown they
wear ($\sigma\tau\acute{\epsilon}\phi\alpha\nu o\varsigma$) suggests that they
attained to these heights of power

through long effort and conflict. Moreover our Lord gives repeated hints that
wider and ever wider spheres of rule
await developing man. 'Thou hast been
faithful over a few things, I will make
thee ruler over many things.' 'The
joy of the Lord' into which the faithful
ones enter is the joy of work. According to their capacities will be the extent
of their rule. 'Have thou authority
over ten cities' is said to one, while
to another is given the charge of five.
Again, the disciples are warned that the
Powers above watch carefully the use
which is made of the limited and temporary authority entrusted to men here
on earth, and according as it is used
selfishly or unselfishly, they withhold
or impart the larger and more indepen-
dent authority which is ready for those
whose characters enable them to use
it well. 'If ye have not been faithful
in the unrighteous mammon who will
commit to your charge the true riches,

and if ye have not been faithful in that
which is another's who will give you
that which is your own?' Again,
the promise to the Apostles (referred
to above), that in the Palingenesis (by
which we may perhaps understand the
beginning of a new 'age' or 'civilization') they should under Himself be its
rulers and guide its destinies, might
well lead us to think that humanity—
using the word in its widest sense to
include not only developing man of
to-day but also the great civilizations
of the past—is placed by God under the
Supreme rule of its 'Elders,' who have
long ago broken free from the 'bondage
of mortality' and who now from their
thrones in the eternal sphere rule
the world. These would be the true
'Kings of the earth,' of whom St. John
tells us that the Incarnate Son of God
is the 'Ruler' (ch. i. 5). If this be so,
we may find in the dual function which
they, the Supreme Guardians of the

race, fulfil, the explanation of the 12×2, and the indication of the twofold path of secular rule and priestly service by which they severally attained to their transcendent authority. 'Thou leddest thy people like sheep by the hand of Moses and Aaron' seems like a key which will fit the lock and explain the mystery. If what has been said about the twelve fundamental types of humanity be true, then we may find in the song of the four and twenty Elders in ch. v. 9 and 10, an explanation in their own words of the question who they are. Instead of supplying, as the translators have done, the word 'men' we may paraphrase the passage thus :—" *No type is unrepresented among those whom thou hast purchased and hast raised to kingship and priesthood, and they shall reign on the earth.*" The important thing to notice is that the functions of both kingship and priesthood are combined. The Elders act as priests and rule as kings. The group around the throne is a ' Royal Priesthood ' *in excelsis.* Humanity has ever a double outlook, towards the secular and towards the spiritual, and they who lead it and represent it and stand for it in either direction are always its true rulers. Yet a true king and a true priest must never be an alien. He must be one of those whom he represents. He must be an ' elder ' among them. Hence if there be twelve fundamental types of humanity we can understand why on the heavenly thrones there must be four and twenty elders sitting.

The number, often repeated, of 144 presents no real difficulty. Each of the twelve tribes or types supplies its full quota of 12,000, making in the aggregate 144,000 (ch. vii. 4). Similarly the 12 trees by the river in the Holy City (xxii. 2) supply 12 manner of fruits, each tree yielding its fruit every month. To say that each of the complete number

of tribes makes its own large contri-
bution, and that a complete supply is
provided of all that is needed for the
changing wants of each of these types,
seems to exhaust the symbolical meaning of these examples of 12 × 12.

In chapter xx. we have several allusions to a period of 1000 years. This
presents a hazardous problem, millen-
nial and perennial, and one which has
been responsible for much writing which
is both fanciful and absurd. Of one
thing we may be quite sure, that the
figure, while referring to a long-extended
period of time, is not meant to be
definite. If we ask, then, Are there any
such long periods extending over many
generations recognizable in history and
referred to in Scripture, the answer
must, I think, be an emphatic affirma-
tive. The stupid mistranslation of
συντελεία τοῦ αἰῶνος as the 'end of
the world' instead of the 'close (or
consummation) of the age' is responsible

for obscuring this as well as much else
in our Lord's teaching. I have written
elsewhere on this subject [1] and need
only say here that such ' ages ' or ' civilizations,' whose beginnings and endings
can be clearly recognized in the perspective of history, have been in the
past, that our Lord gave His followers
the signs by which the close of an age
might be recognized, that such an age
closed and a new age began with the
fall of Jerusalem, and that the age which
began then gives every indication to-
day of hurrying to its close. I would
suggest, then, that it is to just such a
period that the references to a thousand
years in chapter xx. apply.

The number 10, which occurs several
times, presents a greater difficulty. In
each case it has some connexion with
evil. The Christians of Smyrna are to
suffer persecution 10 days. The Dragon,

[1] See p. 24.

the Beast of the Sea, and the Scarlet
Beast have each 10 horns. After the
great earthquake in chapter xi. 'the
tenth part of the city fell.' Perhaps we
may hazard the suggestion that the
number is a combination of 6, which is
the number of the Beast, and 4, to signify
the limitation of his power to the sphere
of the temporal.

Again, if the 42 months (ch. xiii. 5),
during which it was given to the Beast
to make war upon the followers of the
Lamb, stood alone we might be tempted
to think it the product of 6×7, in-
volving the numbers characteristic of
each, but it seems better to regard it
as identical with the 'time and times
and half a time' (ch. xii. 14), i.e. $3\frac{1}{2}$
years or 1,260 days (ch. xi. 3). In the
$3\frac{1}{2}$ itself, 'The broken seven,' we can
trace the influence of evil, but perhaps
that is all we can safely say.

I have left to the last the considera-
tion of the remarkable verse, ' Here is

Wisdom ; He that hath understanding
let him count the number of the Beast,
for it is the number of a man, and his
number is six hundred and sixty and
six' (ch. xiii. 18). It seems to me that
we may safely exclude all interpretations
which seek by ingenious manipulation
to fit the number to the name of Nero,
or Napoleon or any one else. The
wisdom to which St. John appeals is
not the ingenuity involved in a guessing
competition. The Apocalypse does not
deal with particular earthly events or
historic personages, but with the great
moral forces and tendencies which lie
behind them, and with spiritual conditions applicable to every age and
place. A striking illustration of this is
given in chapter xi. 8, where the Seer
speaks of ' the great city which spiritually is called Sodom and Egypt, where
also their Lord was crucified.' There
is no localizing that. It is typically
apocalyptic. It is the vision of the

6

human conditions which involve the Crucifixion of Love, and it is as near to London and Paris and New York as to imperial Rome.

There are two great figures and forces which dominate a considerable part of this book. They are potent, antagonistic, and they control the actions and lives of men. They are τὸ θήριον, the Wild Beast, and τὸ ᾽Αρνίον, the Lamb. The former stands for the spirit of Selfishness, grasping, greedy, cruel, self-assertive. It represents what we mean by the slang phrase ' Number One.' It is graphically painted in Watts' picture of Mammon, and is manifested historically in individuals and in nations.

The Lamb, on the other hand, stands for the spirit of Self-Sacrifice, giving and pouring forth its life. We cannot, of course, separate in thought the spirit of self-sacrifice from its historic and perfect manifestation in Christ. St. John always sees Christ in it, and it in

Christ, and therefore, again and again,
it stands for Christ. Yet essentially
the figure is the abstract spirit of self-
sacrifice standing over against the abstract spirit of selfishness and greed.
Each has his kingdom in the world of
men, and each sets his mark upon his
followers. The Kingdom of the Beast
is widespread and age-long. His system
is organized, his policy is persecution.
No man is allowed to buy or sell unless
he has the mark or the number of the
Beast in his forehead or in his right
hand (unless, that is, he adopts ' business ' plans and ' business ' practices).
Now it has been pointed out by the late
Dr. Milligan that 6 is taken as the
symbol of that which falls short of
perfection as symbolized by 7. The
number is repeated three times ' accord-
to the number of a man,' i.e., according
to his threefold nature, his actions, his
desires, his thoughts.[1] So the mean-

[1] Cf. Our Lord's parable describing the working

ing seems to be that the great distinction between the followers of the Lamb and those who worship the Beast is just the distinction between those who in action, desire, and thought aim at the highest and those who are content to take the 'average' as their standard.   When a man aims not at holiness but at respectability, not to be like Christ, but to be 'no worse than his neighbours,' when he neglects an acknowledged duty on the ground that he 'does not profess to be a saint,' such a man has taken sides and his number 666.   The difference between 777 and 666 may seem very small, yet there could not be a truer application of the poet's words :—

O the little more, and how much it is !
And the little less, and what worlds away !

One who aims at the highest and strives

of the Kingdom of Heaven in man from within till thoughts, desires and actions are dominated by it, as leaven works in '*three measures of meal*' till all is leavened. St. Matthew xiii. 33.

after holiness always feels the sense of
sin and the need of a Saviour. One who
makes 6 his number and aims at the
average becomes self-satisfied and cen-
sorious and does not trouble about his
sins. To aim at the highest means to
raise the average ; to aim at the average
means to lower it. The difference between 7 and 6 seems very small, but
symbolically and spiritually it determines
whether a man is reckoned among the
followers of the Lamb or has placed
himself in antagonism to His claims.

The Sealed Book

IV

The Sealed Book

WHATEVER the Sealed Book may represent, all will admit that to miss or mistake its meaning must involve the darkening as with a fog a considerable part of the Book of Revelation. It is the first formidable problem which faces the student of the Apocalypse. A modern explanation, which is accepted by Archbishop Benson, is that it stands for the 'Book of Destiny.' 'It is,' says Dr. Swete, 'the Book of Destiny, to be unrolled and read only as the Seals are opened by the course of events.' It seems to me that it would be hard indeed to find a more unsatisfying solution. Why should St. John weep much because no one in heaven or earth is found worthy to know in advance what is going to happen, especially if the only way of reading the future is by waiting till the Seals are opened ' by the course of events ' ?   And how is it possible to interpret the series of visions which follow upon the loosing of the Seals, the procession of the Four Riders, the cry of the souls beneath the Altar, and what follows, in terms of events which are to happen in the future ?

On the other hand, we know that there was one problem as old as the world which was pressing at this period with terrible severity on the consciousness of the infant Church—a problem great enough to be worthy of finding a place in the august surroundings of St. John's Vision—the age-long problem of suffering.   The Kingdom of Christ had been proclaimed.   His was the kingdom and the power and the glory.   Why then these bitter persecutions and these cruel martyrdoms ? It was this sense of the need of the vindication of the Cause of Christ which rendered the problem so acute, but the difficulty itself widened out till the whole great question of suffering was embraced, the great woe of the world, the groaning and travailing of creation in pain together from the beginning until now.

If then we take the Sealed Book to represent the problem of the existence of suffering in the world and the toleration of the sin which lies behind so much of it, we have at least an explanation of its meaning worthy of the tremendous and universal challenge. How fittingly too and inevitably the problem arises at the close of nature's great anthem of praise in chapter four ! The pain of nature ' red in tooth and claw,' the anguish of man here and the cry for vindication from the world beyond refuse to be ignored.

We can understand St. John's tears

at the sight of a problem seemingly as
insoluble as it is insufferable. And then
how wonderfully and completely the
development of the vision supplies the
explanation ! There is one solution and
one only to the problem of suffering.
It is solved by self-sacrifice. ' The Lion
of the tribe of Judah . . . prevailed to
open the book.' One has been found
whose strength has triumphed. ' And
I saw,' says St. John, ' in the midst of
the Throne and of the four living creatures and in the midst of the Elders a
Lamb standing as though it had been
slain.' The extraordinary conception of
the strength of the lion manifested
through the weakness of the lamb is
as convincing as it is dramatic. ' My
strength,' says our Lord, ' is made perfect in weakness.' The aorist (ἐνίκησεν),
in the words, ' The lion . . . prevailed,' show that the reference is to a
past event, and therefore to Calvary.
St. John had stood there and had

seen the whole vast problem of human suffering and of the mysterious power of sin represented in epitome in the Cross. He had heard the great cry of dereliction, and seen the darkening of the world. Yet the power and malignancy of sin is not the dominating thought which clings to the Crucifix. It might have been expected that it would for all ages stand as the hideous memorial of the power of hate. On the contrary, it remains for ever the supreme manifestation of the love of God. ' *So* God loved the world.' Its message is not, ' See what sin can do,' but ' See what Love can bear and yet go on loving,' and the terrible force of evil manifested in the Cross only magnifies the mightier power which transformed it into the emblem of divine love. Thus the whole problem is solved by self-sacrifice, and the Lamb alone is worthy to take the Sealed Book out of the hand of Him who sitteth on the Throne.

In instituting the great Sacrament of the Eucharist our Lord taught the same lesson. According to a great and universal law form on earth is ever being broken, life is ever being outpoured. In lower nature—including lower human nature—the operation of that law is being violently resisted. Each creature seeks, whatever the cost to others, to preserve its own form unbroken, its own life from being poured forth. But our Lord taught His followers that they would find the true path to bliss not in resisting but in accepting that universal law. He took the Bread and said, 'This is My Body,' and with His own hands He broke it. He took the Cup and said, 'This is My Blood,' and with His own hands gave it to them; and having thus taught them that in self-sacrifice is Salvation, He said, 'This do in remembrance of Me.'

Taking then the Sealed Book to represent the great 'Why?' of a suffering

world, as well as of a persecuted Church,
we find that the development of the
vision as the Seals are opened fits such
a solution in every particular. The
subject has been dealt with fully on
pp. 139–145, and it may be sufficient
to say shortly here that the opening of
the first four Seals deals with the
causes of suffering on earth in which the
lower creation shares, and traces them to
the selfish use of power in the person of
the rider who goes forth in search of
conquest (ἵνα νικήσῃ). The fifth Seal deals
with the cry for vindication of the
martyrs and the answer they receive.
The sixth reveals with what tremendous
power the cause of God is vindicated
against His enemies when death breaks
up for them the only world they counted
real, and they behold the face of Him
that sitteth on the Throne and feel the
wrath of the Lamb. It shows next that
all destructive forces are held in the
strong hands of God's angels, and that

no harm can really happen to the servants of Jesus at the hands of ' them
that kill the body and after that have
no more that they can do.' Finally,
by the vision of the bliss of the redeemed,
it makes plain that this ' light affliction
which was but for a moment ' had worked
for them ' an exceeding great and eternal
weight of glory.' The opening of the
seventh Seal brings this part of the vision
to a close in Heavenly silence.

Evil in Three Worlds

VI

Evil in Three Worlds

THE PROBLEM OF THE DRAGON
AND THE TWO BEASTS

EVERY student of the Apocalypse
must have noticed the frequent
references to three regions, the heavens,
the sea, and the earth. That the words
are symbolically used there can be no
reasonable doubt, and on a right answer
to the question of their meaning the
intelligibility of the book largely depends. I propose here to make a suggestion, and then to test its applica-
bility to one specially difficult passage.
There are three worlds in which the
consciousness of man may be centred,

the mental, the emotional, and the
physical; the world of thought, the
the world of feeling or desire, and the
world of action. The world of 'things'
is not more real than the world of
desires, or the world of thought. Man
has that in him which enables him to
respond to the vibrations of all three.
Now I suggest that in the technical
phraseology of the Apocalypse the earth
is taken as the symbol of the world
of action; the sea, with its constantly
changing conditions—and is there any
emotion which man can feel which
cannot be mirrored there?—is used as
representing the world of desire; while
the heavens, with its greater and lesser
lights, stands for the world of thought.
Thus St. Luke records a very remarkable Apocalyptic saying of our Lord
referring to the close of an age, 'There
shall be signs in Sun and Moon and
Stars, and upon the earth distress of
nations in perplexity for the roaring

of the sea and the billows ' (St. Luke
xxi. 25). The words are obviously symbolical, but how full of meaning they become when we understand that the sign
upon earth is restlessness among the
nations, and that this is due to great
waves of emotional disturbance and
passion which sweep over the hearts of
men, and that this in its turn follows
upon abnormal developments in the
mental world. Now let us take one
very interesting section of the Book of
Revelation to test this theory. I refer
to the twelfth and thirteenth chapters
which describe—if our theory be true
—the manifestation of evil in the three
worlds of thought, desire, and action.

' Evil,' says an early writer, ' grows
on good like rust on steel.' The manifestation of good seems to have the
power to attract, concentrate, and finally,
after being strengthened by the struggle,
to overthrow the opposing evil. In the
heaven world then, the region of plans

and purposes and thoughts, a great
sign appears. 'A woman clothed with
the sun and the moon under her feet
and upon her head a crown of twelve
stars ; and she was with child : and she
crieth out travailing in birth, and in
pain to be delivered.' If we thus take
the heavens with the greater and lesser
luminaries as representing in Apocalyptic language the mental world, it
would seem that the subject of the
Vision was the manifestation of the
Divine purpose to raise mankind by
the Incarnation of Jesus Christ and by
His Coming to the world as Son of Man.
We are carried back to the great parable
of Genesis, which records the beginnings
of humanity. There we find the same
dramatis personæ referred to in the
words which tell how the seed of the
woman shall bruise the serpent's head.

It will be observed that evil shows
itself as soon as the Divine purpose
is manifested and at once sets itself

to oppose and thwart it. The woman crowned with twelve stars represents humanity in all its twelve types just as the Jewish Church did. The words, ' She was with child,' refer to the purpose of God revealed in the mental world before it became actual in history. The twelve stars emphasize the fact that as Son of Man the Christ represents not one race, but humanity in all its completeness.

During the long process of the working out of God's design in the call of Abraham and the organization of the representative race in twelve tribes and in its long and troubled history, the dragon makes ready for his great assault. Then when the hour comes he strikes at the Christ first through His physical Body in Herod's attack at Bethlehem, then through His desires and thoughts in the Temptations in the wilderness, then through His Will in the Garden of Gethsemane. With the Ascension of the

Christ, the Child of Humanity, the Son of Man, is ' caught up to God to His Throne,' and the woman who as the Church, now organized under the twelve Apostles, still represents complete humanity, flees into the wilderness, the symbol for temptation and trial, and is there nourished for the period symbolized by a ' time and times and half a time.' It is no more possible to change this into a definite period of years than to localize ' the wilderness ' in a definite place. No one who at all understands the nature of the Apocalypse would attempt to do either.

Now let us look specially at the way in which evil manifests itself in this Vision. First it appears in the mental world under the form of ' a great red dragon.' ' There was seen another sign in heaven.' He captures and draws after him ' a third part of the stars of heaven.' Evil takes its origin in the world of intellect and presses into its service a portion of its forces, but it can never keep its foothold there. The higher forces of that world are roused into opposition and there is ' war in heaven.' ' Spiritual wickedness in heavenly places' struggles to retain its foothold and struggles in vain. It is ever being cast out—the process is continuous—the evil thought is ever being transmuted into an evil desire, and the desire in its turn becomes an evil deed and so perishes in pain. ' The lust when it hath conceived beareth sin, and the sin, when it is full-grown, bringeth forth death' (St. James i. 15). Under this process evil is perishing everlastingly. When cast out of the heaven world it is on its way to destruction, hence a great voice is heard in heaven saying, ' Rejoice ye heavens, and ye that dwell in them. Woe for the earth and for the sea, because the Devil is gone down unto you having great wrath because he knoweth that

he hath but a short time' (Rev. xii. 12).
We may compare with this another
Apocalyptic saying of Christ, of which,
according to Dr. Sanday, it is not too
much to say that a large part of the
Book of Revelation is just an expansion,
'I beheld Satan fallen as lightning from
heaven' (St. Luke x. 18) Evil then
while originating in the mental worlds
is never allowed to abide there. It is
cast out and descends to the world
represented by the sea and the earth,
where naturally we should expect to
find fresh manifestations. Accordingly
we read that the dragon stands 'upon
the sand of the sea,' and out of the sea
comes a wild beast monstrous, vile, cun-
ning, fierce and grasping. It is the
hideous abstract figure of Selfishness in
the world of Desire, and the Dragon—
for evil in all three worlds is linked and
kin—gives him his power and his throne
and great authority. Debased intellect
places its undoubted power at the service

of sinful desire. It is always the evil thought which calls forth the evil passion. The wild beast sets up his kingdom among men. Selfishness ever makes the largest claims to authority. He points to the Kingdoms of the world and says, ' That is delivered unto me and unto whomsoever I will I give it.' He demands from men the recognition of his supremacy as he demanded it from Christ. Those only refuse to worship ' whose names are written in the book of life of the Lamb that hath been slain from the foundation of the world.' Those only escape the snare whose lives are unselfishly spent for others.

So much for the manifestation of evil in the worlds of thought and desire. We now anticipate, if our theory be true, its manifestation in the world of action. Accordingly the Seer tells us, ' I saw another wild beast coming up out of the earth ' (ch. xiii. 11). Before we proceed farther it will be well to ask ourselves, How should we expect Selfishness to manifest itself in the world of action as contrasted with its manifestation in the world of desire ? Should we not at once say that it would take on a disguise ? That the silversmiths of Ephesus would develop a quite extraordinary enthusiasm for the worship of Diana, that trickery would describe itself as ' business methods,' and lust masquerade under the name of love. Those are precisely the lines on which the Vision develops. In the beast of the earth all the outward characteristics of ferocity so abundant in the first beast disappear. The ten horns are replaced by two, and these are the horns of a harmless lamb. Instead of the voice speaking great things and blasphemies from the lion-mouth, he speaks ' as a dragon ' or serpent. It is a voice of soft sibilants which suggests the words, ' Yea, hath God said, ye shall not eat of every tree of the garden ? '

(Gen. iii. 1). That 'The Dragon' and 'The Serpent' may in this connexion be regarded as interchangeable and that the verse just quoted must have been in the writer's mind is evident from ch. xii. 9, and from ch. xx. 2, in both of which he speaks of 'The Dragon, the old Serpent' (ὁ ὄφις ὁ ἀρχαῖος). It is important to establish this point, as two highly competent commentators take a very different view. Dr. Swete, enlarging on the somewhat meagre data given in the words ἐλάλει ὡς δράκων, speaks of the voice of the second beast as 'the roar of a dragon.' But is there any authority outside Grimm's Fairy Tales for suggesting that a dragon roars? Assuredly the serpent, which, if not identical with it, may at least claim to be next of kin, has no such power. Nor does the combination of the harmless lamb-like head with 'the roar of a dragon' make for sense or congruity. Dr. Charles, again in his *Studies in the*

Apocalypse, page 101, finds great difficulty in the clause ' and he spake as
a dragon.' ' There are ' he says, ' no
means of explaining it. A dragon does
not speak.' That is true, but is it not
recorded in the great parable of the
Fall in the passage quoted above that
' the old serpent ' did speak ? And does
not St. John identify that ' old serpent '
with the dragon ? And does not the
fact that there is only one such utter-
ance recorded make it practically certain that it was of that subtle and slimy
sentence that the Seer was thinking ?
The words as they stand make excellent
sense. And it would seem to be very
' superfluous ' for Dr. Charles to operate
upon them in the way he does with all
the skill of a conjurer. He translates
the passages into Hebrew, then he
makes certain ingenious and conjectural
changes upon them in that language.
Then he re-translates the passage into
Greek, producing the result, ' But he

was a destroyer like the dragon.'
'Satan,' he says, 'was *the* Apollyon,
but the second beast was *an* Apollyon.'
Thus all that has been accomplished,
by a process which must be considered
very hazardous, is to rob the beast of the
earth of half his disguise.

So far everything in the vision seems
consistent with the belief that we are
dealing with the manifestation of evil
in the three worlds of thought, desire
and action. In each case the form and
manifestation is entirely appropriate.
The dragon from the heaven world
places his authority and power at the
service of the beast in the world of
desire, and he in his turn controls the
actions of men through his disguised
agent the beast of the earth. This
latter exercises 'all the authority of
the first beast in his sight' and causes
the dwellers on the earth to worship
the first beast. Selfishness has its
origin in the world of thought, its home

in the world of desire, and its sphere
of activity in the world of action.   There
the beast of earth dominates commerce
and compels all 'the small, and the
great, the rich, and the poor, the bond
and the free' (note the number 6) to
adopt in their plans and practices the
methods of the first beast and so to
receive his mark in the forehead or the
right hand.   'He causeth that no man
should be able to buy or sell save he
that hath the mark, even the name of
the beast or the number of his name.'
The number of his name is 666, and
as 7 represents the perfect ideal, so 6
stands not for the highest but for that
which we may call the 'average' standard, something necessarily lower than
the highest.

If then we are right in thinking that
these two chapters contain a revelation
of the manifestation of evil in the three
worlds, we can see at once its high practical value.   The early Church knew

only too well that on the side of the
oppressor there was power and that
selfishness seemed to be supreme.   What
they needed to see was its limitations
and its essential weakness and the whole
purpose of the Apocalypse was to reveal
to men, as far as human imagery and
human language would allow, what life
and the problem of life look like when
seen from the spiritual side.

8

The Second Death

VI

The Second Death

IN the previous chapter it was suggested that the Seer of the Apocalypse recognizes three worlds in which the consciousness of man is already active: the physical, the emotional, and the mental. Our correspondence with the physical world depends of course upon our possession of a physical body endowed with senses which enable the consciousness to respond to the vibrations of that world. Now it is unquestionable that our consciousness likewise responds to vibrations from the emotional world and from the mental,

and it would seem to follow that this
would not be possible unless we pos-
sessed some kind of bodies composed
of finer substance and capable of acting
as vehicles of communication with those
worlds. We know that scientists postulated the existence of ether because they
realized that there must be a medium
for the vibrations of light, and it is only
to continue the same lines of thought a
little farther to postulate the existence
of a medium for the vibrations of emotion compared with which medium
ether itself is dense, and another, which
would of course be finer still, for the
vibrations of thought. Cf. references to
this by St. Paul —ψυχικόν (σῶμα), πνευμα-
τικόν—ἐπίγειον.

During our life on earth the consciousness, though through the emotional and
mental bodies so postulated it has a
certain range of activity in these worlds,
yet is centred in the world which we call
physical, and therefore the experiences

we gain from that world we call '*real*'
or '*objective*,' while we term those which
have their origin in the other worlds
'subjective.' Macbeth's dagger, for example, was indeed 'a dagger of the
mind,' but it was *not* therefore necessarily 'a false creation,' as Lady Macbeth
called it. The guilty Thane could not
'clutch' it with his hand, and yet had
he laid aside the physical body by the
simple act of dying, might not that same
'dagger of the mind' have been at least
as visible, ay, and to some subtler grasp
than that of the physical hand been
sufficiently tangible as well ? The poten-
tial objectivity of the subjective is a
matter well deserving more careful study
than it has so far received. For consciousness is not destroyed at death,
but transferred. By putting off the
physical body, we of course lose touch
with the physical world, but if what
we suggested be true, the consciousness
simply transfers its centre to the subtler

body, which brings it into living contact with the emotional world.

What the experiences in that world will be would depend entirely on the nature of the desires entertained in this. The building up of even our physical bodies is far more under the control of the will than is generally realized. They are continually changing the particles of which they are composed—giving out and absorbing, moment by moment. By means of pure food, pure water, and pure air, and healthy exercise we can build up a body which is vigorous and strong, and at every point in joyful contact with the physical world. On the other hand, by neglecting the rules of health, by impure food and foul air, we can so poison the blood, which is the life, that the body becomes a collection of physical discords and jarring discomforts, and we move about the physical world with difficulty and in pain.

It seems quite reasonable from a scientific point of view to believe that in a precisely analogous way it is given to us to build up by the desires we entertain the emotional body to which at death our consciousness is transferred. Let us take two extreme cases. Here, let us suppose, is a man who is continually brooding on what is vile. He listens eagerly to what is evil. He has 'eyes that cannot cease from sin.' He gives free rein to every passion, he stimulates and gratifies natural cravings and creates others which are artificial, using his body meanwhile as the instrument through which these desires, gaining strength from day to day, find their gratification. Every such desire contributes to build up in him an emotional body, tuned, so to speak, only to respond to vibrations which are evil. Imagine the kind of world with which such a man after putting off the physical body at death would find himself surrounded.

What was subjective to him before would become objective now. His surroundings would be of the nature which his own past desires had created for him. As inevitably as a stone sinks to the bottom of the sea so would such a psychic body pass to surroundings in which it would find itself terribly at home. The man in dying would carry with him all the desires and cravings which had mastered him in the days of the flesh, which he had stimulated and gratified, but he would leave behind him the body through which alone they could find their gratification. It is clearly with this problem that our Lord deals so solemnly and so vividly in His parable of the rich man and Lazarus. In it He draws a picture of a man abandoning himself to luxury, served by others, ' clothed in purple and fine linen and faring sumptuously every day.' Then he dies. His tyrant cravings accompany him into the world beyond, but his slaves are all left behind. What can be the condition of one so torn by the old desires while he has no longer got a body by means of which they can be gratified but one of long continued anguish? 'I am tormented,' he says, 'in this flame.' The flame undoubtedly refers to the sense cravings which he had stimulated and gratified in the past and which must go on tormenting him until in course of time they burn themselves out in pain. The fuel of evil imaginations with which these flames have been supplied will in course of time be consumed. It is just this lesson that the wise Greeks taught their people in the myth of Tantalus and that Dante dwells on in his picture of the Gluttons in the Purgatorio sitting famished but penitent round the great tree whose tempting fruit hanging beyond their reach made hunger like a flame. Of course man's sojourn in that psychic body is no more permanent than his stay in the physical body on earth : from it, too, he must in due course pass, but the process by which it is gradually put off must be in such a case as we have been considering one long terrible experience. It is compared in this book to being cast into a lake of fire. Now is it not this putting off of the psychic or desire body which is referred to as ' the Second Death,' just as the First Death is the parting from the body which is physical ?

Again, let us take the case of a man who not only mortifies the desires and deeds of the body and holds its appetites in strong control, but who deliberately ' sets his affections on things above.' He dwells on and longs for what is beautiful and pure and holy. Every such aspiration builds up for him a psychic body which responds only to what is good, and his horror of evil drives it far from him. Here and still more hereafter man gravitates toward the

object of his desires. When at the first
death he passes from the physical body
he will naturally and inevitably then
find himself surrounded by a world of
beauty and purity and light. As surely
as a cork rises to the surface of the ocean,
so surely will he pass to surroundings
with which his affinities lie. As he rises
Heavenwards, his putting off of the
emotional body—for he, too, undergoes
the second death—will be rapid and
painless. He has never while on earth
provided the fuel on which the flames of
fierce desires can feed. He overcame
temptation ere he passed from the
physical world, and having overcome
'he shall not be hurt of the second
death.' Over such 'the second death
hath no power.'

Summary and Explanation of
Chapters iv.—viii. 1.

VII

Summary and Explanation of Chapters iv.—viii. I

SUMMARY OF CHAPTER IV

THE Seer is 'in the Spirit,' i.e., his consciousness is centred no longer in the physical world, but in the spiritual world, which at once interpenetrates and transcends it. The basis of his vision is Heaven, and he sees as the Angels see. From this standpoint he is conscious first of the Divine Throne and the Divine Presence, next of the subordinate Thrones of the great Powers who rule the world for God, then Creation becomes visible as the glassy sea, and lastly the four living Creatures in whom its diverse activities are manifested.

He sees with the eye of the Poet and the Mystic. The language is necessarily symbolical, but it is not really obscure.

He is aware first of a Central All-permeating Life, a Power beyond all power, conscious, controlling, manifesting in and through others but always in Himself complete, always 'Holy, Holy, Holy,' the Everlasting God, dwelling in 'The light that no man can approach unto.' His symbol is the flashing of the blood-red sardine stone, His aureole the emerald bow.

Next the Great Celestial Powers are revealed who from their lower Thrones by delegated authority rule the world for God and through whom His power goes forth, the true 'Kings of the Earth,' clothed in white raiment, and crowned with golden crowns, emblems of spotless purity and kingly power. Then follows the vision of the material universe, ' as it were a glassy sea before the Throne.' As seen from the spiritual side it appears one great bright ocean, reflecting in its ever-changing forms the thoughts of God, and yet in spite of its incessant changes filled with peace deep and profound—

> ' Eternal peace abiding at the heart
>   Of endless agitation.'

So nature must ever seem when viewed from the side of Heaven. But the life that fills it breaks everywhere into consciousness. The One Life reveals itself through the many, and the lower creation sees with its myriad eyes and it lives and rejoices. All that is symbolized by the four Living Creatures.

The basis of the classification is Eastern and superficial, but it is obvious enough. Conscious life on earth divides itself into the Fierce (the lion), the Strong (the ox), the Intelligent (with the face as a man's), and the Swift (the flying eagle).

Through His conscious Creatures the joy of Creation goes up like a great anthem of praise to God. Nature in all its vast harmonies of colour, and form and sound praises Him. The sunset sky, the silver shining of the sea, the rushing of the cataract, the voice of many waters, the murmuring of the wind, and all the multitudinous sounds of life are just so many notes in that tremendous harmony which receives its expression and interpretation more and more fully through higher and higher beings till all is gathered up in the great Benedicite of Nature.

'They have no rest day and night, saying, Holy, Holy, Holy is the Lord God, the Almighty—which was, and which is, and which is to come.' Finally the joy which fills the conscious creation is expressed and offered by its Kings and Priests.

'And when the living creatures shall give glory and honour and thanks to

Him that sitteth on the Throne, to Him that liveth for ever and ever, the four and twenty Elders shall fall down before Him that sitteth on the Throne and shall worship Him that liveth for ever and ever, and shall cast their crowns before the Throne saying, Worthy art Thou, our Lord and our God, to receive the glory and the honour and the power : for Thou didst create all things, and because of Thy will they were and were created.'

SUMMARY OF CHAPTER V

The fourth chapter closes with the great anthem of Creation as expressed and offered by the four and twenty Elders before the Throne of God. Then ere the echo of that praise has died away the fifth chapter opens with the revelation of a dark mystery. A jarring note is introduced, more intolerable because of the grandeur of the harmony, a blot

blackened by the glory of the celestial
light, a tangled thread marring the whole
gorgeous pattern. The vision of the
sealed book represents a profound truth.
Is there no discord in the harmony of
nature ? What of the shriek of the
startled beast as the crooked claws
pierce its flesh ? What of the growl
of fierce satisfaction in the strong ?
What of the pain and anguish of man,

> ' Who trusted God was love indeed
> And love creation's final law,
> Though nature red in tooth and claw
> With ravine shrieked against his creed ? '

All the mute appeals of suffering creation, all the questioning of man, gathered
up in the great ' Why ? ' of Calvary,
tell us the meaning of the sealed book.

So a shadow falls across the bright
vision of the Seer. An explanation is
demanded of the seemingly insoluble,
insuperable, insupportable mystery of
sorrow, pain and death. That is the

sealed book of the vision and the age-long problem of the world. It is not ignored. It is held in (or on) the right hand of Him who sits on the Throne, and that itself is a promise of a solution. Still there is only silence in response to the Challenge of the strong Angel, who proclaims with a loud voice, ' Who is worthy to open the book and to loosen the seals thereof ? ' ' And I wept much,' says the Seer, ' because no one was found worthy to open the book or to look thereon.' ' And one of the Elders saith unto me, Weep not, behold the Lion that is of the tribe of Judah, the root of David, hath overcome, to open the book and to loosen the seven seals thereof.' St. John looks to see some mighty manifestation of strength,— ' The Lion . . . hath overcome.' ' And I saw,' he says, ' . . . a Lamb.' It is the revelation with tremendous dramatic power that God's ' strength is made perfect in weakness.' It explains why

the two scenes in the Incarnate Life
which have laid firmest hold on the
imagination of Christendom are those
of the Infant Christ in His Mother's
arms and the Crucified nailed and helpless upon the Cross.   There is a strength
which the world does not recognize in the
Infant Arms; there is a power which is
not earthly power in the pierced hands.

St. John's thought goes back to
Calvary (note the aorist in ἐνίκησεν ὁ
λέων).   He remembers how the powers
of evil gathered and grew, approaching
and encircling the Christ, then con-
centrating and striking their terrible
blow, and being themselves shattered by
the stroke.   Evil is broken before the
passive strength of the Crucified.   So
the shadow that had fallen on the
Seer's vision takes the sublime form of
the Cross, and St. John saw and understood.   He had seen the historical Crucifixion; now he sees the Eternal Truth
of which Calvary was the reflection

under conditions of time and space.

So the Lamb to whom all power is given in Heaven and earth and who possesses all-comprehending vision approaches and takes the book out of the right hand of Him who sitteth on the Throne.

As He takes the book there bursts forth once more the combined chorus of Earth and Heaven. The four Living Creatures and the four and twenty Elders prostrate themselves in adoration before the Throne. The song they sing is a new song, fuller and grander than before; to the theme of Creation there is added the praise of Redemption.

'Worthy art Thou,' they sing, 'to take the book and to open the seals thereof : for Thou wast slain, and didst purchase unto God with Thy Blood [men] out of every tribe and tongue and people and nation, and madest them to be unto our God a Kingdom and Priests ; and they reign upon the Earth.' From

the Living Creatures and the Elders
the worship spreads to the innumerable
company of the Angels around them,
who take up the song and with a great
voice offer a sevenfold ascription of
praise, saying, ' Worthy is the Lamb that
hath been slain to receive the power and
riches and wisdom and might and honour
and glory and blessing.' And again the
song of the Angels is caught up by the
whole of Creation as the worship widens
and spreads until every created thing
finds a voice and joins in the universal
chorus.

' Unto Him that sitteth on the Throne
and unto the Lamb, be the blessing, and
the honour, and the glory, and the
dominion for ever and ever.' ' And the
four Living Creatures said, Amen. And
the Elders fell down and worshipped.'

CHAPTER VI.

The great ' Storm of Praise' has
passed and the opening of the seven

seals begins. As each seal is loosed the
contents of the book are manifested in
a series of living pictures. The first
four deal with the problem of suffering
as it is felt on earth and shared in by
the lower creation. It is all vision.
The scenes are flashed on the inner
sight of the Seer. As each of the first
four seals is broken he hears one of the
four Living Creatures cry in a voice of
thunder, ' Come.' And in answer to
the call there passes across the stage
of his vision a symbolical representation
of the four great causes of the world's
affliction. Each one inevitably bringing the next one in its train ; Selfish
Ambition, War, Famine, and Death. As
the first seal is opened, ' I saw,' says St.
John, ' and behold a white horse and
he that sat thereon had a bow and there
was given unto him a crown and he
came forth conquering and to conquer,'
or rather ' *in search of conquest.*' The
figure is wholly evil, and the cause of the

evils which follow. It is the personification of Selfishness on a colossal scale when it has acquired power. It manifests itself in a hideous egotism and lust of conquest. He passes, and on the call of the second Living Creature there appears the figure of the rider on the red horse to whom is given a great sword and the power to take peace from the earth,—the dread figure of War.

The third thunder-cry, 'Come,' ushers in in a necessary sequence the rider on the black horse of Famine, bearing the beam of a pair of balances in his hand, and that his identity may not be mistaken the Seer hears from among the four Living Creatures a cry of protest against hunger, a pleading request that a day's work may provide a day's sustenance and that a limit may be set to want.

He, too, passes. Once more a voice cries 'Come,' and the last grim symbolic figure enters, the rider on the pale horse. His name is Death, and he is followed by Hades and his shadowy Kingdom.

So this part of the vision closes. It will be noted that it carries us just as far as the problem of suffering affects the four Living Creatures who represent animate nature. The problem of suffering in so far as it reaches beyond death is dealt with later. The opening of the first four seals reveals only the four-fold woe of earth in which the whole creation, as St. Paul tells us, shares ' groaning and travailing in pain together until now.'

The opening of the Fifth Seal carries us into a region into which the consciousness of the four Living Creatures can no longer follow. No voice any longer cries ' Come,' but St. John sees underneath the Altar ' the Souls of them that had been slain for the word of God and for the testimony which they held.' The problem of suffering

was complicated and intensified for the
Early Church by the need they felt
that the cause of God and the power of
God should be vindicated. Why should
there be no sign of His intervention
when His servants were tortured and
slain ?

'While the sky that noticed all makes no dis-
    closure,
  And the earth keeps up her terrible composure.'

It is an old problem, but it was felt very
acutely then, and the need was great
for an answer and for a revelation of
what it all looked like as seen by ' larger
other eyes than ours.' So the cry with
a great voice from beneath the Altar
gave expression to the question which
was torturing many a heart.

' How long, O Master, the holy and
true, dost Thou not judge and avenge
our blood on them that dwell on the
earth ? '

The answer is very significant. A
white robe, symbolizing a purified char-

acter, is given to each martyr as though
to bid them all realize that while on
earth men fix their attention on outward *circumstances*, in Heaven all is
valued by measuring its effect on *character*. While the friends on earth gather
mourning round the mangled body of
the martyr, the Angels joyfully surround the martyr himself purified by
the suffering which he has endured.
They are told that their cause is not
forgotten and that their vindication
will not fail. They are to rest for a
little longer till the number of those
who are still to suffer should be complete.

The opening of the Sixth Seal brings
before the Seer a twofold vision : the
first part reveals what in the region
beyond physical death is the experience
of the wicked, while in striking contrast
the second part makes evident the
protecting care with which the righteous
are guarded, and their blessed con-

dition before the Throne of God.   Both
messages were needed by the Early
Church.   In those days of bitter persecution it was inevitable that the old
problem, 'I have seen the ungodly in
great power,' should be troubling the
minds of many.   As the Sixth Seal is
opened the world of the wicked is broken
up as by a mighty earthquake.   The
physical world, which alone has seemed
real to them, falls in ruins as the consciousness is forced to awaken to spiritual
realities.   In the blaze of judgment light
the very sun seems to become black as
sackcloth of hair.   All that has before
seemed firm and stable, the very stars
as the symbols of permanence, become
in contrast to the eternal things like so
many unripe figs cast to ground when
shaken by a mighty wind.   The earth
and the heavens as they have known
them pass from their consciousness which
is absorbed by one tremendous vision,
of the infinite Power, the omnipotent

Will, the awful Holiness against which
they have been dashing their puny
efforts. Every faculty is concentrated
on ' The steady Whole of the Judge's
Face,' and their one thought is refuge,
anywhere, in any corner or crevice of
their shattered world.

' Hide us,' they cry, ' from the Face
  of Him that sitteth on the Throne,
  and from the Wrath of the Lamb :
  For the great day of their wrath is come ;
  and who shall be able to stand ? '

That is the vision in which sin, so bold
and brazen here on earth, so apparently triumphant, meets with its utter
overthrow.

It is surely at least lawful to believe
that to immortal beings that tremendous
experience must be the beginning of a
conscience which will ever thereafter
associate opposition to the cause of
righteousness with a sense of horror,
though the experience itself may remain
buried in the subconscious memory.

10

CHAPTER VII

After the revelation of the way in which opposition to God, which on earth for a time seems triumphant, will meet with its final check and overthrow, the Seer witnesses the second part of the twofold vision which follows the opening of the Sixth Seal, and which makes plain how completely the Divine protection guards here and hereafter the followers of JESUS. ' After this,' he says, ' I saw four Angels standing at the four corners of the Earth that no wind should blow on the Earth, or on the sea, or upon any tree.' Then an Angel rising from the East, having in his hand the Seal of the living God, bids them restrain the tempestuous forces under their control till the servants of God are sealed in their foreheads. The winds here obviously represent agencies of destruction ready to break forth upon the world but yet held in strong

control by God's Angels. But what is
the meaning of the protecting seal ?
Dr. Charles, in his interesting commentary on this chapter, rejects the
'practically universal' reply of commentators that it means preservation
from physical evil, and also Düsterdieck's
view that it refers to security against
spiritual apostasy, and suggests instead
that it must be read in connexion with
ch. ix. 4, and that it deals solely
with security against demonic agencies.
But it is surely quite unnecessary to see
more in the words than a promise as
general and inclusive as that of the
Master to His followers when describing
the sufferings which were coming upon
the earth He said, ' There shall not an
hair of your head perish.' The meaning is practically identical with that of
the passage, ' Then shall He send forth
the Angels and gather the Elect from
the four winds.' He did not promise
security from physical danger who said,

' Fear not them that kill the body and *after that* have no more that they can do.' The *bodies* of his followers might be tortured and slain, but they who wore them would be shielded with the most complete protection.

St. John hears the number of those that are sealed and finds that each one of the twelve tribes of the spiritual Israel representing the twelve funda-mental types of humanity contributes its complete quota of 12,000. The number is obviously mystical and signifies completeness. That he is not meant to understand it otherwise is immediately made plain, for after hear-ing the numbers there breaks upon his view a vision in which the company of the mystical hundred and forty and four thousand expand into ' a great multitude which no man could number out of every nation and of all tribes and peoples and tongues.' They stand ' before the Throne and before the

Lamb clothed in white robes and palms
in their hands, and they cry with a great
voice, saying, Salvation unto our God
which sitteth on the Throne and unto
the Lamb. And all the Angels were
standing round about the Throne and
about the Elders and the four Living
Creatures ; and they fell before the
Throne on their faces and worshipped
God, saying, Amen : Blessing, and glory,
and wisdom, and thanksgiving, and
honour, and power, and might, be unto
our God for ever and ever. Amen.'

The chapter closes with a passage of
wonderful beauty and deep spiritual
meaning. ' One of the Elders answered,
saying unto me, These which are arrayed
in the white robes, who are they and
whence came they ? And I say unto
him, My Lord, Thou knowest. And He
said to me, These are they which come
out of the great tribulation, and they
washed their robes and made them white
in the blood of the Lamb.' What is

'the great tribulation'? Dr. Charles insists that it is 'wholly inadmissible' to give the words a general signification. They must, he thinks, be taken to refer to a particular epoch of persecution. But surely that depends entirely on the standpoint of the speaker. It is not St. John who uses the phrase, but the mighty Spiritual Being who talked with him. From the comprehensive heaven point of view the long trial of earthly life may well be described as 'the great tribulation' from which new additions to the innumerable multitude keep ever coming. As seen from earthly life, where we depend so much on the bodily senses, the followers of Christ are scattered from one another far and wide, and they are divided by death: from the side of heaven, in whatever condition or in whatever world they may be, they are seen as one mighty host. They are the selfless ones. They have opened their hearts to others, and in the outgoing tide of divine life and love flowing from within their own characters (robes) have been cleansed and made pure and white. Because of this they are before the Throne of God and serve Him day and night in His Temple. Wherever they may be, in the heaven life or working for Him here on earth, out of the physical body, or in it (and may not that be the Heavenly One's meaning of ' day and night ' ?) they are ever ' before the Throne of God,' in the conscious realization of His Presence, carrying out the work appointed for them.

> ' They do God's will : to them all one
> Or in the Earth or in the Sun.'

And their God is ever with them and in them. ' He that sitteth upon the Throne shall spread His Tabernacle over them '; through the lowest of earthly slums, through the vilest surroundings, they can pass unharmed, undefiled as

the rays of God's own sunlight. They
bear ever with them and around them
the protecting atmosphere of the Divine
Presence. Desire which binds others
to this world has ceased for them. They
use the things of earth, but are not held
by them. ' They shall hunger no more,
neither thirst any more.' No one who
lives consciously in the spiritual world
can ever value for their own sake worldly
things. The world wearies its votaries
and disappoints them, but these pass
through it unwearied and unscathed.
' Neither shall the sun strike upon them
nor any heat'; their desires are raised
above the things which can never satisfy
and set on spiritual things where the
supply is illimitable. ' For the Lamb
which is in the midst of the Throne shall
be their Shepherd and shall guide them
unto fountains of water of life, and God
shall wipe away every tear from their
eyes.'

CHAPTER VIII. 1

It is impossible to dissociate the verse which describes the solemn and dramatic silence which follows the opening of the Seventh Seal from the words in Genesis which tell of the completed work of Creation, 'And on the seventh day God ended His work which he had made, and he rested on the seventh day from all His work which He had made.'

The opening of the Seventh Seal, like the sounding of the Seventh Trumpet and the pouring forth of the Seventh Bowl, marks the completion of all that has gone before. It seems quite as unnecessary to seek for a further significance in the Silence of Heaven as to seek for it in the rest which followed upon the Creation

Commentary on Chapters i.-vii.

VIII

Commentary on Chapters i.-vii

I. 1 THE revelation of Jesus Christ
which God gave him to show
unto his servants, even the things

1 'The revelation of Jesus Christ.' The unveiling of the great spiritual realities which lie
behind the changing things of this life.
This unveiling is made by Jesus Christ.
'Which God gave him to show,' etc. Cf. St.
John xvii. 8, 'The words which Thou gavest
me I have given unto them.'
'The things which must shortly come to pass.'
They who have seen the architect's plans
can tell how the house will be built. They
who have seen the realities of the spiritual
world can tell what the reflections will be
like.
'He sent and signified it by his angel.' An
Angel at Christ's command impresses on

which must shortly come to pass ; and
he sent and signified it by his angel
2 unto his servant John : who bare
witness of the word of God, and of
the testimony of Jesus Christ, even
3 of all things that he saw. Blessed
is he that readeth and they that hear
the words of the prophecy and keep
the things which are written therein,
for the time is at hand.

the   soul-sight of St. John the series of
visions which make up the book.
‘To His servant John.’   Through His more
advanced servants He teaches the younger.
2 ‘Who bare witness of the word of God and of
the testimony of Jesus Christ.’   That is
the   revelation contained   in   this   book.
The   visions came   from   God, they   were
witnessed to by Jesus Christ, they were
seen by St. John.
3 ‘Blessed is he that readeth and they that
hear,’ etc. Public reading is referred to,
and a blessing is pronounced on those who
pass on to others the teaching of the book
and on those who hear it and keep it.
‘The time is at hand.’ The realities which
St. John had seen when ‘ in the Spirit ’

4   John to the seven churches which
    are in Asia : Grace to you and peace,
    from Him which is and which was
    and which is to come ; and from
    the seven Spirits which are before
5 his throne ; and from Jesus Christ,
    who is the faithful witness, the first-
    born of the dead, and the ruler of
    the kings of the earth. Unto him

would, he knew, rapidly materialize on
earth.

4 ' To the seven churches,' etc.   Primarily to the
    seven churches named, but it is evident
    that in a mystical book like the Apocalypse
    the seven churches are collectively taken
    as representing the whole Church.

' From him which is,' etc.   The unusual form of
    the salutation (ἀπὸ ὁ ὤν) has a parallel in,
    ' say that I AM hath sent you.'

' From the seven Spirits,' etc.   From the Holy
    Ghost.   The presence of these words in the
    salutation   exclude   any   lesser   meaning.
    Their unusual position seems to be due to
    the instinctive desire of St. John to dwell
    on the Name and attributes of Jesus Christ.

5 ' Jesus   Christ,   the   faithful   witness.'   The
    Visible Witness by His Incarnation of the
    Great Unseen Spiritual world.

that loveth us and loosed us from
our sins by his blood ; and he made
6 us to be a kingdom, to be priests

'The firstborn of the dead.' The first of
    humanity to rise through physical death
    to full and perfected manhood in Heaven.
    The Resurrection is not a return to earthly
    conditions but a rising out of them. The
    recall of Lazarus to the physical world was
    in no sense a resurrection, but rather a
    movement in the opposite direction.
'The ruler of the kings of the earth.' The
    real Kings of the Earth are the throned
    and crowned ' Elders ' of humanity whose
    sovereignty under God was revealed to
    St. John (chap. iv. 4).
'Unto him that loveth us,' etc. The mention
    of the Name of Jesus calls from the heart
    of St. John a great rush of devotion.
    We can almost see the eyes raised to Heaven
    and the glow of love on his face.
'And loosed [or cleansed] us.' The Jewish
    Law and Ritual aimed at impressing
    constantly on men the sense of sin.
'By his blood.' By the outpouring of His
    life (or blood) which the Cross made manifest
    to the world.
6 'A kingdom,' i.e., a nation or company of
    Kings. Humanity, as it develops, takes

unto his God and Father ; to him
be the glory and the dominion for
7 ever and ever. Amen. Behold he
cometh with the clouds, and every
eye shall see him, and they which
pierced him ; and all the tribes of
the earth shall mourn over him.
Even so. Amen.
8   I am the Alpha and the Omega,

on the double functions of kingship and
priesthood. Cf. 'Ye are a royal Priesthood' (1 St. Pet. ii. 9).

7 'Behold he cometh with clouds,' etc. St.
John is quoting musingly two Old Testament prophecies, blending them together
and thinking how wonderfully they are
fulfilled in the great Coming of the Son of
Man to the world which took place at
Pentecost. (See p. 37 et seq., where the
meaning of this verse is fully discussed.)

'With clouds,' i.e., veiled from worldly sight,
'not with observation.'

'Even so. Amen,' i.e., how complete the
fulfilment !

8 'I am the Alpha and the Omega.' 'The phrase,'
says Dr. Swete, ' is seen to express not eternity only, but infinitude, the boundless life
which embraces all while it transcends all.'

11

saith the Lord God, which was, and
which is, and which is to come, the
Almighty.

9 I John, your brother and partaker
with you in the tribulation and kingdom and patience which are in Jesus,
was in the isle that is called Patmos,
for the word of God and the testi-

'Saith the Lord God.' Swete attributes the
words to God the Father, but there seems
no sufficient reason why they might not be
spoken by Jesus Christ, who in chap. xxii. 13
applies to Himself the words, 'I am the
Alpha and the Omega.' The words that
follow, 'Which is, and which was, and
which is to come, the Almighty' [or All-
Ruler] are applicable to both God the
Father and God the Son. Cf. v. 17.

9 'Your brother and partaker with you,' etc.
The love of St. John for his people and
his own great humility instinctively led
him to describe himself in words which
identify himself with them.

'In the tribulation and kingdom.' Cf. 'If
we suffer we shall also reign with Him.'
To endure tribulation brings with it the
power of influence over others. To rule

10 mony of Jesus. I was in the Spirit
on the Lord's day, and I heard behind
me a great voice, as of a trumpet say-
11 ing, What thou seest, write in a book

over the hearts of men one must wear a
crown of Thorns.

' Was in the isle that is called Patmos, for the
word of God,' etc. An exile during the
persecution. The persecutors no doubt
sent him there to isolate him and remove
his great influence. God overruled their
purpose and made his exile the means of
rendering his influence world-wide and
age-long.

10 ' I was in the Spirit.' I *became* in the Spirit.
I passed into a condition in which I saw
and heard from the Heaven side, remaining
entranced to bodily experiences.

' On the Lord's day.' A very early Christian
phrase for the first day of the week.

' I heard behind me a great voice as of a trumpet.' Suddenly as though he heard it
with his outer ear a voice, clear as a trumpet,
strikes on his consciousness from an unseen source behind him. It is the voice of
the Hierophant or Angel Guide.

11 ' What thou seest, write in a book,' etc. The
statement of the divine purpose which lay
behind his exile.

and send it to the seven churches;
unto Ephesus, and unto Smyrna,
and unto Pergamum, and unto
Thyatira, and unto Sardis, and unto
Philadelphia and unto Laodicea.
12 And I turned to see the voice which
spake with me.   And having turned
I saw seven golden candlesticks ; and

'To the seven churches.' The message to
the seven chief churches of Asia Minor
forms the basis of the vision.   The Apocalypse, like Jacob's ladder, reaches to
Heaven : these cities form the spot at
which it touches earth.
12 'I saw seven golden candlesticks.' Dr. Swete,
after his usual custom, speaks of the Seer
having taken one feature of this vision
from 1 Kings vii. 49, and another from
Exodus xxv. 36 and Zechariah iv. 2.
'Our writer,' he says, '*more suo*, takes
from each source the features which lend
themselves to his conception.' One may
protest against his repeated assumptions
that St. John did not see these visions at
all, but merely concocted them, borrowing
scraps from previous writers and so making
up a patchwork document.

13 in the midst of the candlesticks one
like unto a son of man, clothed with a
garment down to the foot, and girt
about at the breasts with a golden gir-
14 dle. And his head and his hair were
white as white wool, white as snow ;
and his eyes were as a flame of fire ;
15 and his feet like unto burnished brass
as if it had been refined in a furnace ;
and his voice as the voice of many

13 ' In the midst of the candlesticks.' Manifesting
his Presence with them.
' One like unto a son of man.' A human form.
' A garment down to the foot.' A priestly robe.
' A golden girdle.' Perhaps to suggest royalty.
14 ' His head and his hair were white as white
wool.' There is no suggestion of age in
this description. The whiteness is in
accordance with the heavenly splendour of
the manifestation.
' His eyes were as a flame of fire.' Eyes rapid
and piercing in their glance and glowing
with eternal life.
15 ' His feet like unto burnished brass,' etc.
Translucent like glowing metal.
' His voice as the voice of many waters.' Multitudinous, comprehensive, far-extending,
with deep and wonderful harmony.

16 waters. And he had in his right hand seven stars : and out of his mouth proceeded a sharp two-edged sword, and his countenance was as
17 the sun shineth in his strength. And when I saw him I fell at his feet as one dead. And he laid his right hand upon me, saying, Fear not ;
18 I am the first and the last, and the

16 'In his right hand seven stars.' Many things can be clearly seen in a vision which cannot be reproduced in a picture. The meaning is plain. The right hand gives protection and imparts power.

'Out of his mouth proceeded a sharp two-edged sword.' An Eastern can think in symbols and does not seek to correlate them into one picture as the Western does.

'His countenance was as the sun shineth in his strength.' As once before St. John had seen Him in the Holy Mount.

17 'I fell at his feet as one dead.' Cf. Daniel viii. 27 and 2 Corinthians xii. 7 and 8. The frail physical body is not tuned to respond to mighty spiritual vibrations.

'He laid his right hand upon me.' Imparting the strength. Cf. Daniel x. 18.

18 'Fear not ; I am the first,' etc. 'I dwell

Living one ; and I was dead, and
behold, I am alive for evermore, and
I have the keys of death and of
19 Hades. Write therefore the things
which thou sawest, and the things
which are, and the things which
shall come to pass hereafter ; the
20 mystery of the seven stars which

in the eternal and the real. I entered
the life of earth, and passed through it,
and became dead ; I passed through the
gate of death into Hades and through the
gate of Hades into the Heaven world.
The lower worlds are open to Me. Therefore
because I, having passed through them,
speak with the authority of experience,
Write,'

19 'Write therefore.' Write of the lower life
as it is seen from the higher.

'The things which are, and the things which
shall come to pass hereafter.' 'The things
which are' are the thoughts in the Eternal
Mind visible in the Heaven world. They
materialize or 'come to pass on earth.'

20 'The mystery of the seven stars . . . candlesticks.' The candlesticks or lampstands
are the Churches as seen and known on

thou sawest in my right hand, and
the seven golden candlesticks. The
seven stars are the angels of the
seven churches: and the seven
candlesticks are seven churches.

II. 1   To the angel of the church in
Ephesus write ;

> earth, one at Ephesus, one at Smyrna, etc.
> The stars are the Churches as seen and
> known from a higher level. Thus a man
> is seen and known on earth by his body,
> but from the Heaven world he is seen and
> known by his spiritual counterpart or
> Angel (cf. St. Matt. xviii. 10 ; Acts xii. 15),
> and is visible not by face and form and
> feature, but by desires and thoughts. The
> Angels of the Churches bear the same
> relation to the Churches that a man does
> to the body he wears.
>
>   The vision brings a double comfort.
> The Churches on earth as seen from
> Heaven have in their midst the Presence
> of the Christ. The Churches themselves
> are beyond the reach of the attacks of
> earthly foes. Like stars, they are in the
> right hand of the Living Christ in the
> place of protection and the place of power.

1 ' The church in Ephesus.'   Ephesus was large,

These things saith he that holdeth
the seven stars in his right hand,
he that walketh in the midst of the
2 seven golden candlesticks : I know
thy works, and thy toil and patience,
and that thou canst not bear evil
men, and didst try them which call
themselves apostles, and they are
3 not, and didst find them false ; and
thou hast patience and didst bear
for my name's sake, and hast not
4 grown weary.   But I have this against
thee, that thou didst leave thy first

important, cosmopolitan, thriving, a trad-
ing centre, the home of the worship of
Diana, given to practices of magic and
such like cults.

'These things saith he . . . candlesticks.'
He who is present in His Church and who
guards and strengthens its life.

2 'I know thy works,' etc. It is like Christ
first to look for and dwell on what is good.
He acknowledges hard work patiently done,
the conflict with pseudo-Apostles, the quiet
and steady orthodoxy.

4 'But . . . thou didst leave thy first love.'
The first fervour and zeal had passed away.

5 love.   Remember   therefore   from
    whence thou art fallen and repent
    and do the first works ;   or else I
    come to thee, and will move thy
    candlestick out of its place, except

All outward observances were maintained,
but rather as the continuance of a tradition than as the expression of devotion.
Cf. Matthew Arnold's words—

> ' Its form still stood without a breach,
> When life and warmth were fled,
> And still it spake its wonted speech,
> But every word was dead.'

The Church at Ephesus was living on its
spiritual capital.

5 ' Remember therefore,' etc.   Remember, Repent, Do.

So Cowper's question—

> ' Where is the blessedness I knew
> When first I saw the Lord ? '

leads to—

> ' I hate the sins that made Thee mourn.'

' Do the first works.'   The love will come in
doing the loving deeds—so Jesus taught—
and renewed life will come with love.

' Or else I come to thee, and will move thy
candlestick,' etc.   The Church at Ephesus

6 thou repent. But this thou hast,
that thou hatest the works of the
7 Nicolaitans, which I also hate. He
that hath an ear let him hear what
the Spirit saith to the churches. To
him that overcometh, to him will I
give to eat of the tree of life, which
is in the midst of the Paradise of God.

was perishing, as all self-centred Churches
must. Only by doing the first loving works
and opening its heart to others could it
receive from within the supplies of life
to save itself.

6 'But this thou hast,' etc. The instinctive
tact of Divine love closes with commenda-
tion and suggestion of affinity.

The Nicolaitans were a sect who seem
to have taught people to ignore the restrictions laid down for Gentiles by the
decree of the Council at Jerusalem. Such
a course of action in a place where heathen-
ism was dominant would almost certainly
lead to laxity of morals wholly unworthy
of the Christian standard.

7 'He that hath ears,' etc. So the message
to the local church becomes world-wide
and age-long.

'To him that overcometh.' This book is

8   And to the angel of the church in
Smyrna write ;

These things saith the first and
the last, which was dead and lived

> written in a time of crisis and struggle, and
> hence all its promises are to victors. The
> conflict is not less real now, though less
> apparent.

'To him will I give to eat of the tree of life,'
etc. As the body grows by food, so our
spiritual nature expands by assimilating
truth. The truths of the Heaven world
are the food by which immortal man lives.
Those who overcome the allurements of
the world and give themselves to God
are granted from time to time the power
to grasp and make their own some great
truth which is the fruit of the tree of
life—such knowledge once gained is never
lost, but endureth to everlasting life.'

8 'The church in Smyrna.' It was a Church
distressed, poverty-stricken, persecuted,
and especially by Jews, and fresh trials
were impending. Its needs were, to obtain
a true perspective, to be rescued from the
absorbing power of the present distress,
and to see it all against the background of
immortality : hence,

'These things saith the first and the last.'

9 again : I know thy tribulation, and thy poverty (but thou art rich), and the blasphemy of them which say they are Jews, and they are not, but are a

'The Everlasting Arms go all round.' The persecution will become a memory. Trouble passes, kings and kingdoms change—Christ remains, and they.

'Which was dead and lived again.' Death for them as for Him is but an incident in life.

9 'I know thy tribulation.' The sympathy of Christ would remove the bitterness of the feeling so common in times of great trial. 'Then I said, God hath forgotten . . . He will never see it.' He who in His own sorrow said 'Watch with Me' knew their need.

'But thou art rich.' From the Heaven point of view, those lives only are poor who have no hold on or desire for the true riches. After putting off the body they will be literally destitute whose desires cling to the things of earth from which they are forcibly withdrawn. In Christ's view poverty and riches depend not on what we have but on what we are.

'A synagogue of Satan.' So far may a divinely appointed society fall. The true Israel

10 synagogue of Satan. Fear not the things which thou art about to suffer: behold, the devil is about to cast some of you into prison, that ye may be tried ; and ye shall have tribulation ten days. Be thou faithful unto death, and I will give thee the crown

11 of life. He that hath an ear, let him hear what the Spirit saith to the churches. He that overcometh shall not be hurt of the second death.

was represented by the remnant who had accepted Christ.

10 'That ye may be tried.' Attention is called to God's motive in allowing the persecution, not to the Devil's motive in bringing it about.

'Ten days.' A considerable period, but yet limited.

'Unto death.' Be ready to lay life down. Cf. 'Fear not them that kill the body and *after that* have no more that they can do.'

'The crown of life.' The fear was loss of life. The message of Christ is that life is gained not lost by being laid down.

11 'He that hath an ear, let him hear.' To some this will sound unintelligible, but

12 And to the angel of the church in Pergamum write;

13 These things saith he that hath the sharp two-edged sword : I know where thou dwellest, even where Satan's throne is ; and thou holdest fast my name, and didst not deny my faith, even in the days of Antipas, my witness, my faithful one, who was killed among you where Satan

it has a meaning to all whose inner ear is opened.

'The second death.' (See p. 65 et seq., where the meaning of these words is discussed.)

13 'He that hath the sharp two-edged sword.' So the message which is mainly one of warning appropriately begins—

'I know where thou dwellest.' Christ allows for environment. Pergamum was a centre for idolatry. Idolatrous rites were more or less inwoven with all social customs, and questions as to the right attitude of Christians were continually emerging.

'Where Satan's throne is.' The seat of an aggressive and immoral paganism.

'Thou holdest fast my name and didst not deny my faith.' Thou art prepared against

14 dwelleth. But I have a few things against thee, because thou hast there some that hold the teaching of Balaam, who taught Balak to cast a stumbling-block before the children of Israel, to eat things sacrificed to
15 idols, and to commit fornication. So hast thou also some that hold the teaching of the Nicolaitans in like
16 manner. Repent therefore; or else I come to thee quickly, and I

direct assault and in the recent persecution didst reject the temptation to apostasy.

'Antipas, my witness, my faithful one.' What a bond of union a Saint becomes between his fellow-disciples and the Master!

14 'The teaching of Balaam.' There was a chronic temptation for those who mixed in social life with idolaters to lower the standard and to permit without protest the compromises by which prominent Christians were letting their loyalty be sapped The salt must not be allowed to lose its savour.

15 'The teaching of the Nicolaitans.' See note on v. 6.

16 'I will make war against them with the sword

will make war against them with
17 the sword of my mouth. He that
hath an ear, let him hear what the
Spirit saith unto the churches. To
him that overcometh, to him will I
give of the hidden manna, and I
will give him a white stone, and
upon the stone a new name written,
which no one knoweth but he that
receiveth it.

of my mouth.' I will send an Apostle
or one in high authority to denounce and
excommunicate them in My Name. The
Church in Pergamum is thus called on to
exercise discipline.

17 'The hidden manna.' A pot of manna had
been laid up before the Lord in the ark
(Exod. xvi. 23). No one now knew where
the ark was. 'Suddenly, as rare things
will, it vanished.' There is probably in
this promise a reference to the fact that,
as both in public and private feasts food
was offered to idols, loyal Christians were
excluded from partaking, but like their
Lord they could say, 'I have meat to eat
that ye know not of.' Christ Himself
drew near to them, and they received

12

18   And to the angel of the church in Thyatira write ;

These things saith the Son of God, who hath his eyes like a flame of fire, and his feet are like unto burnished

19 brass : I know thy works, and thy love and faith and ministry and patience, and that thy last works

'an hundredfold more, now in this present time.'

' A white stone.' Stones engraved with mystical words or signs were common among the magi and probably were used in the rites from which Christians were excluded. They are promised a spiritual gift instead.

' A new name written which no one knoweth but he that receiveth it.' To every earnest Christian the Name of Christ suggests something which is special and peculiar to himself. As different precious stones reflect in different ways the one light, so each Christian reflects in a way peculiar to himself the character of Christ, and each knows just as much of Christ as he reflects.

18 ' Who hath his eyes like a flame of fire.' Eyes keen to see the motive behind the action.

19 ' Thy love and faith and ministry and patience.' A beautiful combination, and it is combined

20 are more than the first. But I have
this against thee, that thou sufferest
the woman Jezebel, which calleth
herself a prophetess ; and she teach-
eth and seduceth my servants to
commit fornication and to eat things
21 sacrificed to idols. And I gave her
time that she should repent, and
she willeth not to repent of her
22 fornication. Behold, I do cast her
into a bed, and them that commit
adultery with her into great tribulation, except they repent of her works.

with progress. The eyes which are like a
flame of fire see first and see clearly what
is good.

20 ' The woman Jezebel.' Probably some female
teacher with real psychic power and gift
of speech who had taught the lawfulness of
Christians joining in heathen feasts and
had in consequence led some to yield to
temptation to fornication.

22 ' I do cast her into a bed.' Her days of
activity are closing. As vigorous life is
checked when one is laid on a bed of sick-
ness, so her influence for evil shall lose

23 And I will kill her children with
   death ; and all the churches shall
   know that I am he which searcheth
   the reins and hearts : and I will give
   unto each one of you according to
24 your works.   But to you I say,
   to the rest that are in Thyatira, as
   many as have not this teaching,
   which know not the deep things of
   Satan, as they say ; I cast upon

   its power.   And those whom she has
   beguiled shall suffer with her.
23 ' Her children.'   Not so much those who have
   been entrapped by her as those who assist
   her.
   ' The reins and hearts.'   The feelings and the
   will.
   ' Unto each one of you.'   Those who have and
   those who have not gone into error.
24 ' The deep things of Satan as they say.'   These
   false teachers were proud of their knowledge
   of the occult, the ' deep things ' as they
   called them.   ' Yes,' says   the   Christ,
   ' deep things of Satan.'   There is a back
   door into the spiritual world, and the
   practices of necromancy and spiritualism
   are as evil as they are dangerous.

25 you none other burden. Howbeit
   that which ye have, hold fast till I
26 come. And he that overcometh,
   and he that keepeth my works unto
   the end, to him will I give authority
27 over the nations: and he shall rule
   them with a rod of iron, as the vessels
   of the potter are broken to shivers ;
   as I also have received of my Father :
28 and I will give him the morning star.

25 ' That which ye have, hold fast.' Probably
   this refers to the decree of the Council of
   Jerusalem regarding the standard laid
   down for Gentiles.
26 ' He that overcometh and he that keepeth,' etc.
   The words suggest that the victory is only
   gained after a prolonged and perhaps lifelong struggle.
   ' Authority over the nations.' The nations
   who are now hostile shall be brought under
   control and shepherded, while the hostile
   elements in them shall be broken to pieces.
   The cause of Christ is eternal—the opposing
   forces have no permanency.
28 ' I will give him the morning star.' The
   morning star to one who has watched
   through the long night brings the joy of

29 He that hath an ear, let him hear what the Spirit saith to the churches.

III. 1 And to the angel of the church in Sardis write;

These things saith he that hath the seven Spirits of God, and the seven stars : I know thy works, that thou hast a name that thou livest,

a sure and certain hope. It does not materially disperse the darkness but leaves no doubt that the darkness will be dispersed. So the 'earnest of the Spirit' gives a foretaste of bliss and heavenly joy.

1 'He that hath the seven Spirits of God,' i.e., the All-Conscious One. Cf. 'Seven eyes, which are the seven Spirits of God.' ch. v. 6.

'And the seven stars.' In whose power and under whose protection the seven churches are.

'Thou art dead.' As a sleeping man is dead to the material world around him, so the Church at Sardis no longer responded to the realities of the spiritual world. Cf. St. Matthew viii. 22. Their temptation was to maintain an outward activity and

2 and thou art dead. Be thou watchful, and stablish the things that remain, which were ready to die: for I have found no works of thine
3 fulfilled before my God. Remember therefore how thou hast received and didst hear; and keep it and repent. If therefore thou shalt not watch, I will come as a thief, and thou shalt not know what hour I

display of satisfactory statistics while careless about vital religion, a very real danger in many a local church.

2 'Be thou watchful.' They had power to rouse themselves and to become awake and alive to eternal things.

'Stablish the things that remain.' The dying embers can yet be fanned into a flame.

'Which were ready to die.' The words imply expectation that the warning will be heeded. There is yet time to reform, none to lose.

'Fulfilled before my God.' A deed good in itself is defective and lacking before God unless the motive which prompts it is good.

3 'Remember therefore how thou hast received and didst hear.' What you heard at first is an abiding trust. How you heard

4 will come upon thee. But thou
hast a few names in Sardis which
did not defile their garments: and
they shall walk with me in white;
5 for they are worthy. He that overcometh shall thus be arrayed in

should be a constant stimulus and standard.
'Keep it and repent'—and at once. The in-
    junction is vigorous and peremptory.
'As a thief.' Who chooses the unexpected
    moment. Some turn of the wheel of
    circumstances will reveal to all the hidden
    defects of character, e.g., the sudden out-
    break of persecution issuing in a general
    apostasy.
4 'But'—as against all this, and acting as the
    salt in checking this corruption—
'did not defile their garments.' Kept their
    baptismal robes pure from heathen sin.
'They shall walk with me in white.' Here
    and hereafter. When the will is loyally
    turned to God we live in an atmosphere of
    constant forgiveness, dwelling in the cleans-
    ing element of the Divine life as fish in the
    sea.
'Shall thus be arrayed in white garments.'
    As in the Transfiguration the whiteness is
    a glory from within.

white garments ; and I will in no
wise blot his name out of the
book of life, and I will confess his
name before my Father, and before
6 his angels. He that hath an ear,
let him hear what the Spirit saith
to the churches.
7   And to the angel of the church in
Philadelphia write ;

> 'I will in no wise blot his name out of the
> book of life.' The promise implies a solemn
> warning to the rest. Here as elsewhere
> it is important to keep in mind that from
> the standpoint of the Christ 'life' means
> power to respond to the realities of the
> eternal world.

> 'I will confess his name before my Father
> and before his angels.' When the Christ
> life and Christ character are manifested
> towards man in the face of opposition they
> are simultaneously made manifest Heaven-
> wards before God and the Holy Angels,
> or, to state a spiritual reality in parabolic
> form, the Name of Christ becomes written
> on the forehead.

> 7 'He that hath the key of David.' The Jews
> bitterly persecuted their fellow-countrymen
> who had embraced Christianity and treated

These things saith he that is holy,
he that is true, he that hath the key
of David, he that openeth, and none
shall shut, and that shutteth, and
8 none openeth : I know thy works
(behold, I have set before thee a door
opened, which none can shut), that
thou hast a little power, and didst

them as outcasts from Israel. Here the
Christ, Who as Messiah holds all authority
in the true Israel, recognizes and admits
them and excludes their opponents.

8 'I have set before thee a door opened.' The
opened door here seems to refer not to the
admission of the Christian and excom-
municated Jews to the true Israel—their
place within is acknowledged by Christ—
but He has opened for them a door out-
wards to let the Gospel go forth to the
Gentiles.

'Didst keep my word.' Perhaps a reference
to the command of Christ to make disciples of all nations.

'Didst not deny my name.' To have changed
their religion from being an unselfish cause
into a bundle of exclusive privileges would
have been to deny the name and character
of Christ,

keep my word, and didst not deny
9 my name. Behold, I give of the
synagogue of Satan, of them which
say they are Jews, and they are not,
but do lie ; behold, I will make
them to come and worship before
thy feet, and to know that I have
10 loved thee. Because thou didst
keep the word of my patience, I also
will keep thee from the hour of trial,
that hour which is to come upon the
whole world, to try them that dwell

9 ' I give of the synagogue of Satan.' A promise
of conversions from among their enemies—
a glorious revenge.

' Which say they are Jews and they are not.'
Cf. ' They are not all Israel which are of
Israel.'

' That I have loved thee,' or rather ' that I loved
Thee.' The aorist seems to refer to a past
crisis, when outwardly the Church seemed
forsaken.

10 ' The word of my patience.' The patience
of Christ which conquers by enduring,
and sees the triumph beyond the suffering.

' The hour of trial.' There is no suggestion of
anything final in this hour of trial.

11 upon the earth. I come quickly :
hold fast that which thou hast, that
12 no one take thy crown.   He that

11 'I come quickly.' The words here are a
welcome promise ; in other cases a solemn
warning. Christ always comes quickly
to those who have for His sake braved
fiery trial.

'Hold fast that which thou hast.' Only
maintain that attitude of fidelity and
patience. It is the encouraging call to a
runner who has almost secured the prize.

12 'A pillar.' The thoughts suggested are Dig-
nity and Beauty, Permanence, and especially supporting Strength. The strong
pillar keeps in their place a multitude of
lesser stones which, without, it would fall.

'He shall go out thence no more.' He shall
live in the conscious realization of the
Presence of God wherever he may outwardly be. His consciousness shall always
be centred in those spiritual regions which
now in its highest moments it touches.
Cf. St. Augustine's last talk with Monica.

'The name of my God.' I will make his
character God-like. Cf. 'We shall be
like him for we shall see him even as he
is ' (1 John iii. 2).

'The name of the city of my God, the new
Jerusalem.' Excluded from the fellowship

overcometh, I will make him a pillar
in the temple of my God, and he
shall go out thence no more : and
I will write upon him the name of
my God, and the name of the city
of my God, the new Jerusalem,
which cometh down out of heaven
from my God, and mine own new
13 name. He that hath an ear, let
him hear what the Spirit saith to
the churches.

14 And to the angel of the church
in Laodicea write ;

of the old Jerusalem which was the shadow
of the true, they shall bear the mark of
citizenship of the Jerusalem which is
above, and which is in the Church material-
izing upon earth.

'My new name.' Jesus, Saviour, Redeemer.
They, too, will live to save and redeem.
So the promise is complete. He that
overcometh shall be manifested as a Child
of God, a brother to all who love Christ,
and a missionary to all who know Him not.

14 'The Amen, the faithful and true witness.' A
Church so self-satisfied would resent severe

These things saith the Amen, the
faithful and true witness, the begin-
15 ning of the creation of God : I know
thy works, that thou art neither cold
nor hot ; I would thou wert cold
16 or hot. So because thou art lukewarm, and neither hot nor cold, I

criticism from others, but this comes from
Him who sees and knows and cannot
err.

'The beginning of the creation of God,' i.e.,
the fount of Creation, ' by whom all things
were made '—He Himself is uncreated.

15 'thou art neither cold nor hot.' Professor
Ramsay points out that near this city
there were famous hot springs whose waters
became lukewarm ere they reached it, so
the illustration is borrowed from local
conditions.   The people were neither hostile
nor zealous.   Respectability 'heavy as
frost' reigned in Laodicea.

'I would thou wert cold or hot.' Christ's
religion is a cause to be eagerly espoused
or rejected, not to be played with. Cf.
our Lord's words, ' He that gathereth not
with Me scattereth.'

16 'I will spew thee out of my mouth.' Such a
state of things cannot last.

17 will spew thee out of my mouth. Because thou sayest, I am rich, and
have gotten riches, and have need
of nothing; and knowest not that
thou art the wretched one and miserable and poor and blind and naked;
18 I counsel thee to buy of me gold
refined by fire, that thou mayest
become rich; and white garments,
that thou mayest clothe thyself,
and that the shame of thy nakedness
be not made manifest; and eyesalve to anoint thine eyes, that thou

17 'I am rich.' Unlike the Church at Sardis,
the Laodicean Church seems to have
included many wealthy and influential
people.
'Thou art the wretched one.' As seen from
Heaven.
18 'I counsel thee to buy of me.' The price is
penitence, earnestness, and prayer.
'Gold refined by the fire.' Possessions which
will outlive this earth life. Perhaps a
reference to the wealth of Christians which
had bought off persecution.
'And white garments.' A reference probably
to the black woollen garments commonly

19 mayest see.   As many as I love, I
    reprove and chasten :   be zealous
20 therefore, and repent.   Behold, I
    stand at the door and knock : if any

used by the people. The fine garments
they wore did not conceal their moral and
spiritual nakedness from the eyes of
Heaven.   White suggests purity acquired
by self-sacrifice.

'And eyesalve.' Cf. the question of the
Pharisees, 'Are we blind also ? ' (St. John
ix. 40). They were blind from the point of
view of those who see the eternal things.

19 'As many as I love, I reprove.' It was like
Jesus Christ to close a rebuke so severe
with a word of love. Severity which con-
ceals love defeats its own end.

20 'Behold, I stand at the door and knock.' Man
is like a house with two fronts.   On one
side of his being he faces the transitory
world ; on its inner, farther side he looks out
on the world which is eternal. It is from
that eternal world that the Christ approaches
and at the door on that side of our being
He stands and knocks and waits. We must
withdraw the consciousness from external
things and make a silence from the outer
world if we would hear the voice within.
'*Sileant omnes creaturæ, taceant omnes*

man hear my voice, and open the door,
I will come in to him and will sup with
21 him, and he with me. He that overcometh, I will give to sit down with
me in my throne, as I also overcame,
and sat down with my Father in
22 his throne. He that hath an ear,
let him hear what the Spirit saith
to the churches.

doctores, *Tu mihi loquere solus.*' must be
the cry of the soul.
' I will come in and sup with him, and he with
me.' I will enter into all his joys and
sorrows, difficulties and hopes, enterprises
and experiences, and make them mine,
guiding, correcting, and sharing as love
knows how. I will drink his cup—and
he shall drink mine. He shall enter into,
and, as far as he can, make his own all my
enterprises and experiences, hopes and difficulties, joys and sorrows, pouring in his
own supply of energy and love. The power
to share is just equal to the power to love.
The words supply a picture not of union
but of communion, and imply the permanence of the individuality.
21 ' He that overcometh, I will give to sit down
with me in my throne.' The attention,

13

IV. 1 After these things I saw, and behold, a door opened in heaven, and the first voice which I heard, a voice as of a trumpet speaking with me, one saying, Come up hither, and I will show thee the things which must come to pass hereafter.

which is at first turned with effort from the attractions of the world to the Christ Who approaches from within, will later on be turned earthward again to help and bless and rule the world in His Name.

1 'A door opened in heaven.' Not in the sky. Heaven is all around and within. It is opened for those in whom the faculties are awakened which respond to heavenly realities. It is opened as the starry world is opened when the darkness falls. Earth and the things of earth are not excluded from the vision, but all are seen with a wider view and from a new and higher standpoint.

'The first voice which I heard.' The voice of the Angel Guide (i. 10).

'Come up hither.' See things from the Heaven point of view. The change is a change of consciousness, not of movement from one place to another.

2 Straightway I was in the Spirit : and behold, there was a throne set in heaven, and one sitting upon the

' I will show thee the things which must come to pass.' As an architect might show a friend the plan of a building in process of construction. The mental world, which seems to be the ' heaven ' of the Apocalypse, is the repository of the plans of those things which ' must come to pass.'

2 ' Straightway I was (became) in the Spirit.' At once I began to see from the side of Spirit rather than from the side of form. The contrast between the two points of view is worthy of notice. An earth-centred consciousness would first perceive material things, then it would far more dimly recognize living powers behind them, and only finally and very faintly arrive at the idea of a Supreme God. But St. John is 'in the Spirit,' and he therefore sees in the reverse order, beginning first with the Throne of God.

' There was a throne set in heaven.' A Nero or a Domitian might hold sway on earth, but to one ' in the Spirit ' it was plain that beyond and above all Justice reigned and Holiness, and that His was ' the Kingdom, the Power, and the Glory.'

' One sitting upon the throne.' There is deep

3 throne ; and he that sat was to
look upon like a jasper stone and
a sardius : and there was a rain-
bow round about the throne, like
4 an emerald to look upon. And
round about the throne were four
and twenty thrones : and upon the
thrones I saw four and twenty
elders sitting, arrayed in white
garments ; and on their heads crowns
5 of gold. And out of the throne

reverence in the absence of all description.
He clothes Himself with light as with a
garment, and it is the pure and living light
of which earthly gems are a faint reflection.

3 'Like a jasper stone and a sardius . . . emerald.' The ruddy glow of central light
softened by the 'perfect round' of the
emerald green.

4 'Round about the throne were four and twenty
thrones.' The revelation that the world is
ruled for God by great Spiritual Beings is
a truth which has been largely lost sight of.
'Four and twenty elders.' (See p. 85).

5 'Lightnings and voices and thunders.' From
the source of all power proceed energies,
impulses, messages, forces creative and

proceed lightnings and voices and thunders. And there were seven lamps of fire burning before the throne, which are the seven Spirits
6 of God; and before the throne, as it were a glassy sea like unto crystal; and in the midst of the throne, and round about the throne, four living creatures full of eyes before and

destructive. The heavenly thunders have a significance for those who have ears to hear. Cf. ch. x. 4.

'Seven lamps of fire.' A symbol of the presence of energies of the Holy Spirit. Just as there is a certain duality associated with the second Person of the Blessed Trinity, so the number seven appears to be specially associated with God the Holy Ghost.

6 ' A glassy sea.' The world of nature as seen from the Heaven side. Material things are but reflections in three dimensions of the thoughts of God. The reflections appear and pass: the thoughts remain. There is a peace and restfulness in nature in the midst of all its boundless activities like the stillness of the ocean at its centre.

'In the midst . . . and round about . . .'

7 behind. And the first creature was like a lion, and the second creature like a calf, and the third creature had a face as of a man, and the fourth creature was like a flying
8 eagle. And the four living creatures,

The language used to describe things and movements in a world of three dimensions is quite inadequate to enable us to make a mental picture from this and some similar verses. It would need a fourth dimension to afford any realizable conception of the Four Living Creatures full of eyes before and behind and within (v. 8) in the midst of the Throne and round about the Throne. It is better not to make the attempt. The very vagueness has a power all its own, as in Tennyson's remarkable line—

'Great Angels, awful shapes, and wings and eyes.'

Perhaps, too, there is the suggestion of God's consciousness in and through nature, and that every sense in nature may be regarded as an organ of Deity.

7 Animate creation is represented under a four-fold and thoroughly Eastern classification. The fierce, the strong, the intelligent, the swift. Four is the number of earth.

8 'Having each of them six wings.' 'The

having each one of them six wings,
are full of eyes round about and
within : and they have no rest day
and night, saying, Holy, Holy, Holy,
is the Lord God, the Almighty, which
was, and which is, and which is to
9 come. And when the living creatures shall give glory and honour
and thanks to him that sitteth on
the throne, to him that liveth for

> wings . . . represent the velocities of na-
> ture, as the eyes represented its sleepless
> vigilance ' (Swete).
> 'Full of eyes . . . within.' (See note, v. 6.)
> 'They have no rest day and night.' 'All thy
> works praise thee, O Lord.' So the saint
> and the poet realize. In that mighty
> volume of praise there is no pause or rest,
> and the burden of the praise as at length
> it gains expression in God's highest crea-
> tures is ' Holy, Holy, Holy.'
> 9 ' Glory and honour and thanks.' The vision
> of the threefold Majesty of Him who sits
> on the Throne seems to dominate the
> whole chapter and to cast a threefold re-
> flection on its very phrases. Cf. vv. 5, 8. 11.

10 ever and ever, the four and twenty
elders shall fall down before him
that sitteth on the throne, and shall
worship him that liveth for ever and
ever, and shall cast their crowns
11 before the throne, saying, Worthy
art thou, our Lord and our God,
to receive the glory and the honour
and the power : for thou didst create
all things, and because of thy will
they were, and were created.

10 ' The four and twenty elders shall fall down,'
etc.   Just as it needs the poet to find in
the flower ' thoughts that do often lie
too deep for tears ' and to interpret nature
for those less gifted, so here it is the highest
Beings who express and interpret and
turn Godwards the living joy which thrills
creation.   They who from their thrones
rule nature as its kings, become its priests
and make themselves the channels by
which that mighty tide of God-given joy
and praise reaches the throne,

> ' When that which drew from out the boundless
> deep
> Turns again home.'

11 ' They were, and were created.'   The distinction

V. 1 And I saw in the right hand of him that sat on the throne a book written within and on the back, close
2 sealed with seven seals. And I saw a strong angel proclaiming with a great voice, Who is worthy to open the

is very interesting, and is a striking confirmation of Plato's doctrine of ideas. The creation of a flower in the physical world is not its beginning but a projected temporary reflection in the three-dimensional world of a thought or idea which always existed in the Eternal mind which is the *real* world.

1 ' A book . . . close sealed.' The sealed book is the mystery of suffering and the apparent triumph of evil. Why should suffering be allowed, and pain and death ? Why should the saints of God be persecuted and slain ? Why should His cause remain unvindicated ? Why should the oppressors seem to triumph ? Why should they who have fallen asleep in Christ seem to have perished ? This was the problem which was troubling the consciousness of the persecuted Church. The loosing of the seals supplies the answer.

2 ' Who is worthy,' etc. The problem is not ignored, but brought forward for solution.

book, and to loose the seals thereof ?
3 And no one in the heaven, or on the
earth, or under the earth, was able
to open the book, or to look thereon.
4 And I wept much, because no one
was found worthy to open the book,
5 or to look thereon : and one of the
elders saith unto me, Weep not :
behold, the Lion that is of the tribe
of Judah, the Root of David, hath
overcome to open the book and the

3 ' No one in the heaven or on the earth,' etc.
It baffles human wisdom and angelic.
Cf. Eph. iii. 10.
4 ' And I wept much.'   The note of suffering jars
on the ear which has listened to the harmony of creation's great chorus of praise
in the previous chapter.   If it had been, as
some commentators say, 'the Book of
Destiny,' the reason for the Seer's much
weeping would be less obvious.
5 ' And one of the elders saith unto me, Weep not.'
One of the Crowned Rulers who represent
and rule humanity from their thrones in
the Heaven world.
    ' Behold, the Lion that is of the tribe of Judah.'
The problem is cosmic, its solution is made

6 seven seals thereof. And I saw **in**
the midst of the throne, and of the
four living creatures, and in the
midst of the elders, a Lamb standing, as though it had been slain,
having seven horns and seven eyes,
which are the seven Spirits of God,

manifest in history. The reference to the
tribe of Judah is another indication that the
organization of Israel into twelve tribes
represents something permanent and fundamental in humanity (see p. 82).

' Hath overcome,' or rather ' overcame ' (aorist)
' See, the Lion . . . overcame,' in order
that men might see the victory had to be
manifested under conditions of time and
space. ' See, in the Cross the mystery
is at once revealed and solved.'

6 ' And I saw . . . a Lamb.' The Seer looks
for a manifestation of divine strength and
finds it in weakness (cf. ' My power is
made perfect in weakness,' 2 Cor. xii. 9). In
the wounds of Calvary is ' the hiding of
His power.'

> ' 'Tis the weakness in strength that I cry for,
>   my flesh that I seek
> In the Godhead.'
>
> (Browning's ' Saul.')

Seen from the earth side, the Victim of

7 sent forth into all the earth. And
he came, and he taketh it out of
the right hand of him that sat on the
8 throne. And when he had taken
the book, the four living creatures
and the four and twenty elders fell

Calvary was held there helpless by the
nails ; seen from Heaven, the Conqueror of
Calvary held Himself there by the mighty
power of His consecrated Will.

' As though it had been slain.' Death is only
an incident in life. In Holman Hunt's
great picture of ' The Flight into Egypt '
the great sword gash which slaughtered
one of the innocents appears as only a rent
in the little vest he wears.

' In the midst.' The centre of a spiritual
vision is that which absorbs attention.

' Having seven horns and seven eyes.' Plenary
power and omniscience. There is no power
which He cannot overcome and nothing
lies outside His consciousness.

' Sent forth into all the earth.' Cf. ' Go ye
therefore and make disciples of all the
nations . . . and lo, I am with you alway '
(St. Matt. xxviii. 19, 20).

The four living creatures and the four and
twenty elders.' The representatives of
animate Creation join with the Elders

down before the Lamb, having each
one a harp, and golden bowls full
of incense, which are the prayers of
9 the saints. And they sing a new
song, saying, Worthy art thou to
take the book, and to open the seals
thereof : for thou wast slain, and
didst purchase unto God with thy
blood men of every tribe, and tongue,

> of humanity in a burst of praise as the
> problem of suffering passes into the hand of
> One who can solve it. Cf. ' The earnest
> expectation of the creation waiteth for
> the revealing of the sons of God'
> (Rom. viii. 19). This whole passage of St.
> Paul's should be read in this connexion.
>
> ' Having each one a harp and golden bowls.'
> The harps to symbolize praise, the bowls
> of incense to represent prayer and worship.
>
> 9 ' A new song." The Song of Redemption in
> which Creation shares. Cf. ' The Creation
> itself also shall be delivered ' (Rom. viii. 21).
>
> ' Worthy art thou to take the book,' etc.
> The problem of suffering can only be
> solved by self-sacrifice.
>
> ' Thou wast slain.' The Lamb is the type of
> life given, not of life taken. Cf. ' No man

10 and people, and nation, and madest
   them to be unto our God a kingdom
   and priests ; and they reign upon
11 the earth. And I saw, and I heard

> taketh My life from Me, but I lay it down
> of Myself.'

' And didst purchase unto God [men] out of
   every tribe,' etc. See p. 88, where the
   identity of the Elders is discussed. If the
   Elders, as is there suggested, are referring to
   themselves as taken from each of the
   different types of humanity, then the word
   ' men ' as supplied by the translators is
   wrong : if a word must be supplied it
   should rather be ' representatives.'

10 ' A kingdom and priests.' The word ' king-
    dom ' here stands for a company of kings.
    The two functions of kingship and priest-
    hood are combined in the four and twenty
    elders who stand as the representatives of
    humanity according as its energies are
    turned earthwards or Godwards.

' And they reign upon the earth.' Though
   themselves seated on the heavenly thrones.

11 ' I heard the voice of many angels.' The
    worship of Creation as expressed by the
    Elders spreads outwards in great rings of
    praise till it becomes one mighty voice of
    harmony.

a voice of many angels round about
the throne and the living creatures
and the elders; and the number
of them was ten thousand times ten
thousand, and thousands of thousands;
12 saying with a great voice, Worthy
is the Lamb that hath been slain to
receive the power, and riches, and
wisdom, and might, and honour, and
13 glory, and blessing. And every
created thing which is in the heaven,
and on the earth, and under the
earth, and on the sea, and all things

12 'Worthy is the Lamb that hath been slain
to receive power,' etc. The sufferings of
the world come when on the side of the
selfish there is power; but where self-
sacrifice is, there and there only can power
safely be given. The praise because earth
and Heaven combine to offer it becomes
sevenfold.
13 'And every created thing.' The praise now
becomes the universal worship of Creation
'from its four great fields of life' (Swete).
The language grows more general and
the doxology again takes fourfold form.

that are in them, heard I saying,
Unto him that sitteth on the throne,
and unto the Lamb, be the blessing,
and the honour, and the glory, and

14 the dominion, for ever and ever.   And
the four living creatures said, Amen.
And the elders fell down and worshipped.

VI. 1   And I saw when the Lamb
opened one of the seven seals, and
I heard one of the four living creatures saying as with a voice of

14 ' The four living creatures said, Amen.' Creation
has found its place and share in the universal worship.

' The elders fell down and worshipped.'   The
great scene ends with an act of Adoration
in which humanity as represented by its
Elders prostrates itself before the throne.

1 ' One of the four living creatures.'   They have
their share in the groaning and travailing
of creation in so far as the suffering is
confined to this world.

' With a voice of thunder.'   The suffering
often silent on earth sounds in the Heaven
world with a voice of thunder.

' Come.'   Calling the first figure to pass before
the stage of the Seer's vision.

2 thunder, Come. And I saw, and
behold, a white horse, and he that
sat thereon had a bow ; and there
was given unto him a crown : and
he came forth conquering, and to
conquer.

3   And when he opened the second
seal, I heard the second living crea-
4 ture saying, Come. And another

2 ' A white horse,' etc. It is amazing that a
    thinker like Archbishop Benson should
    identify the rider on the white horse with
    Christ. The figure is wholly evil and the
    prime cause of the evils which follow. It
    is the representation of selfishness which
    has grasped the reins of power. It stands
    for a colossal and aggressive egotism.
  ' Conquering and to conquer,' or rather, ' in
    search of conquest.' That is the motive
    of his going forth. The words ' conquering
    and to conquer ' have been so often used
    in connexion with the extension of Christi-
    anity that they have come to acquire in
    popular use a respectable meaning which
    the original will not bear.
4 ' A red horse.' The abstract figure of War.
    The lust of conquest breaks the peace of the

14

horse came forth, a red horse ; and to him that sat thereon it was given to take peace from the earth, and that they should slay one another : and there was given unto him a great sword.

5   And when he opened the third seal, I heard the third living creature saying, Come. And I saw, and behold, a black horse ; and he that sat thereon had a balance in his hand.

6 And I heard as it were a voice in the midst of the four living creatures

earth and draws suffering and slaughter in its train.

5 ' A black horse.' The representation of Famine, which follows the waste and destruction of war as inevitably as war follows the lust of conquest.

' A balance in his hand.' In time of war people are often fed by measure.

6 ' A measure of wheat for a penny,' etc. A pleading voice that a day's wage may be sufficient to procure a day's sustenance. Note how the number 4 appears again in the list of the necessaries of life, wheat, barley, oil and wine.

saying, A measure of wheat for a
penny, and three measures of barley
for a penny ; and the oil and the
wine hurt thou not.

7 And when he opened the fourth
seal, I heard the voice of the fourth
8 living creature saying, Come. And
I saw, and behold, a pale horse : and
he that sat upon him, his name was
Death ; and Hades followed with
him. And there was given unto
them authority over the fourth part
of the earth, to kill with sword, and
with famine, and with death, and
by the wild beasts of the earth.

9 And when he opened the fifth

8 ' A pale horse.' The word translated ' pale '
(χλωρός) means generally grass-coloured,
but here it obviously means the colour of
withered grass. In that scorching land
the period of greenness is comparatively
short.

' And with death.' Used here for pestilence.
Note again the number 4. Cf. Ezekiel
xiv. 21.

9 ' When he opened the fifth seal.' The Living

seal, I saw underneath the altar the
souls of them that had been slain
for the word of God, and for the
10 testimony which they held : and
they cried with a great voice, saying, How long, O Master, the holy
and true, dost thou not judge and
avenge our blood on them that dwell
11 on the earth ?   And there was given
them to each one a white robe ; and

Creatures are silent. The first four seals
deal with causes of sufferings which they
share. The fifth seal carries us into a
region into which the consciousness of the
lower creation cannot follow, and deals
with problems which are no longer theirs.
' Under the altar.'   Thus witness is borne to
the sacrificial character and value of their
offered lives.
10 ' How long.'   There is no doubt in the Master,
the holy and true, but there is the presence
of a problem felt acutely and shared with
the Church on earth, and a deep longing
that the Cause of Christ should be openly
vindicated.
11 ' To each one a white robe.'   The robe is the
Character.   In pouring out their lives

it was said unto them, that they
should rest yet for a little time, until
their fellow-servants also and their
brethren, which should be killed even
as they were, should be fulfilled.

12   And I saw when he opened the
sixth seal, and there was a great
earthquake; and the sun became
black as sackcloth of hair, and the

> the Blood (or Life) of Christ is poured out
> through them. Their sufferings are united
> to His in the great Atoning sacrifice. The
> effect of that outflowing cleansing stream
> upon their own characters is to make them
> white and clean. Character is everything
> with God, and they are bidden to turn
> their attention to that.

> 'They should rest yet for a little time.' Rest
> in preparation for renewed and fuller work.
> For them it is a little time, though on earth
> it may cover a long period or 'age' till
> the martyr roll of the period should be
> complete.

12 The cry for the vindication of right is answered
> by the first vision which follows on the
> opening of the sixth seal. In this tre-
> mendous vision is pictured the experience
> of the enemies of Christ when they shall

13 whole moon became as blood; and
the stars of the heaven fell unto the
earth, as a fig tree casteth her unripe
figs, when she is shaken of a great
14 wind. And the heaven was removed
as a scroll when it is rolled up; and
every mountain and island were
15 moved out of their places. And

be forced to face and realize the awful
holiness and almighty power of the Son of
God. As the consciousness of the wicked is
transferred from physical and transitory
things which alone they thought real to the
great spiritual realities, their world seems
to break up. The sun, which stands for
their ideal of brightness, seems black in
comparison to the blaze of celestial light;
13 the moon, the symbol of beauty, becomes
a horror of blood; and the stars, which
everywhere suggest permanency to man,
are, in view of the eternal things, like so
many unripe figs scattered to earth by a
mighty wind.
14 To a consciousness so shifting, things that
seemed great are swept away, and all sense
of values are violently changed in that dread
vindication.
15 ' And the kings,' etc. A sevenfold list mark-
ing the completeness of the Judgment.

the kings of the earth, and the princes,
and the chief captains, and the rich,
and the strong, and every bondman
and freeman, hid themselves in the
caves and in the rocks of the moun-
16 tains ; and they say to the mountains and to the rocks, Fall on us,
and hide us from the face of him
that sitteth on the throne, and from
17 the wrath of the Lamb : for the great
day of their wrath is come ; and
who is able to stand ?

VII. 1   After this I saw four angels

' Hid themselves in the caves,' etc. Seeking
shelter among the ruins of their shattered
world, hiding from the eternal realities
among the things of time and space. All
the energies of their being are turned into
one fierce desire to escape from the absorbing vision of the Face of the Judge.

16 ' The wrath of the Lamb.' No outrage against
Himself could call from Christ anything
but pity and prayer, but when the weak,
the helpless, are assailed and the innocent
tempted to sin, then Love itself bursts
into flame. That is the wrath of the Lamb.

1 ' The four winds.' Representing destructive

standing at the four corners of the earth, holding the four winds of the earth, that no wind should blow on the earth, or on the sea, or upon any
2 tree. And I saw another angel ascend from the sunrising, having the seal of the living God: and he cried with a great voice to the four angels, to whom it was given to hurt
3 the earth and the sea, saying, Hurt not the earth, neither the sea, nor the trees, till we shall have sealed the servants of our God on their

forces. They are held in control by God's Angels, who have power over the elemental forces of Nature. Four is the number of earth, as three is the number of Heaven.

2 'Another angel.' The angels who have the power to destroy are themselves under a higher obedience.

'Having the seal of the living God.' Cf. Ezekiel ix. 4.

3 'Hurt not the earth,' etc. Cf. St. Mark xiii. 27.

'Nor the trees.' Perhaps the religions of the world.

'Till we shall have sealed,' etc. Cf. 1 Cor. x. 13.

4 foreheads. And I heard the number
of them which were sealed, a hundred
and forty and four thousand, sealed
out of every tribe of the children of
Israel.

5 Of the tribe of Judah were sealed
twelve thousand :
Of the tribe of Reuben twelve
thousand :
Of the tribe of Gad twelve thousand :

4 ' Out of every tribe of the children of Israel,'
i.e., out of the twelve types of humanity of
which the tribes of Israel were in their
turn the type.

5 ' Of the tribe of Judah.' The primacy was
given to Judah, which became the royal
tribe (Gen. xlix. 10). The order in which
the other tribes are given is unusual and
meaningless, but it has been pointed out
by Dr. Buchanan Gray (*Encyc. Bib.*, iv. 52),
that probably vv. 7 and 8 have been
accidentally transposed, and that their
true place is immediately after Reuben's
in v. 5. This would give in order the sons
of Leah, the sons of Rachel, the sons of
Zilpah and the sons of Bilhah.

6   Of the tribe of Asher twelve
thousand :

Of the tribe of Naphtali twelve
thousand :

Of the tribe of Manasseh twelve
thousand :

7   Of the tribe of Simeon twelve
thousand :

Of the tribe of Levi twelve thousand :

Of the tribe of Issachar twelve
thousand :

8   Of the tribe of Zebulun twelve
thousand :

Of the tribe of Joseph twelve thousand :

Of the tribe of Benjamin were
sealed twelve thousand.

6 'The tribe of Manasseh.' Ephraim, to whom
the birthright of the family of Joseph was
given (Gen. xlviii. 20), is already represented
under the name of Joseph. Manasseh is
brought in to take the place of Dan which
is omitted, just as St. Matthias was brought
in to take the place of Judas. The tribe of

9 After these things I saw, and behold,
a great multitude, which no man
could number, out of every nation,
and of all tribes and peoples and
tongues, standing before the throne
and before the Lamb, arrayed in
white robes, and palms in their

Dan seems to have fallen into idolatry
and an early tradition suggests that the
Antichrist was to spring from that tribe.

The twelve thousand sealed from each
tribe is a mystical and symbolical, and not a
definite number. It implies that from each
tribe or type the full quota is supplied.

9 ' A great multitude,' etc. The multitude is but
an expansion of the 144,000 just seen ; it appears now not under its representative types,
but as one united and innumerable band.

' Standing before the throne,' etc. The vision
is not distant and future. As seen from
the spiritual side, those who have gained
the victory over sin and self are ever one
multitude standing before God and the
Lamb wherever they may outwardly be.
They only stand before the throne and
before the Lamb who are Godlike and
Christlike.

' Arrayed in white robes.' With characters
purified.

10 hands ; and they cry with a great
voice, saying, Salvation unto our God
which sitteth on the throne, and
11 unto the Lamb.   And all the angels
were standing round about the throne,
and about the elders and the four
living creatures ; and they fell before
the throne on their faces, and wor-
12 shipped God, saying, Amen : Blessing, and glory, and wisdom, and
thanksgiving, and honour, and power,
and might, be unto our God for
13 ever and ever.   Amen.   And one of
the elders answered, saying unto me,

'Palms in their hands.'   As at the Feast of
Tabernacles at the Temple in Jerusalem.
10 'Salvation unto our God.'   It is the ' Hosanna '
('save now') accompanied by the waving
of palms as in the old days at Jerusalem.
12 'Amen : Blessing and glory,' etc.   The angels
make the chorus to the song of the redeemed and the united worship becomes
sevenfold in form.
13 'And one of the elders answered.'   Replying
to St. John's unspoken desire to know.   In
the Heaven world thought answers thought.

These which are arrayed in the white robes, who are they, and whence
14 came they? And I say unto him, My Lord, thou knowest. And he said to me, 'These are they which come out of the great tribulation, and they washed their robes, and made them white in the blood of
15 the Lamb. Therefore are they before the throne of God; and

14 'These are they which come,' etc. Who keep on coming.

'The great tribulation.' The age-long trial of life on earth.

'They washed their robes and made them white in the blood of the Lamb.' The Life of Christ poured forth through His people for the helping and raising of the world is 'the blood of the Lamb.' It is ever seeking exit through them. Self-seeking sets in motion a force opposite to, and acting as a check on, that outgoing tide.

15 'Before the throne of God.' In the conscious realization of His Presence.

'Shall spread his tabernacle.' God's Presence shall surround them like an atmosphere, and go with them where they go.

they serve him day and night in
his temple : and he that sitteth on
the throne shall spread his tabernacle
16 over them. They shall hunger no
more, neither thirst any more ;
neither shall the sun strike upon
17 them, nor any heat : for the Lamb
which is in the midst of the throne
shall be their shepherd, and shall
guide them unto fountains of waters
of life : and God shall wipe away
every tear from their eyes.

16 'They shall hunger no more, neither thirst
any more.' Desire shall no longer bind them
to the changing things of a changing world.
'Neither shall the sun strike upon them.'
Where desire for temporal things has been
changed into aspiration for heavenly things,
there is no earth-weariness and disappoint-
ment.

17 'Shall guide them unto fountains of waters of
life.' Shall satisfy the infinite longings of
the human spirit with infinite supplies
from the Divine.
'God shall wipe away every tear from their
eyes.' Cf. 'Your sorrow shall be *turned
into* joy' (St. John xvi. 20).

Historic Christianity and the
Mystical Sense

IX

Historic Christianity and the Mystical Sense

THERE have always been in the Christian Church a certain number of people—necessarily a small minority, but a minority of the very best—who have based their belief in the Gospel, less on external testimony than on the inner witness of their spirit. They have held that where through moral effort the spiritual nature reaches a certain level of development, faculties are aroused which respond to the realities of the spiritual world as truly as our bodily senses respond to material things ; and that just as the world of colour and sound would grow round the man born blind and deaf if those faculties in him could be awakened, so all Heaven grows round the man whose inner sense begins to respond to its wonderful and glorious vibrations.

If we place a gold coin in a closed wooden box the ordinary eye will, of course, see nothing but the wood, but under the X-rays the wood which before alone appeared real now seems only a shadow, while the coin invisible before is now seen as the only solid reality.

Let us imagine a number of people endowed with what we might call X-rays sight. They would move about among their fellow-men, yet they would be largely living in a different world. Their actions would seem strange to others and their motives unintelligible. If one of them wrote about the things he saw, his book would be as incomprehensible to the majority as the Gospel of St. John is to the majority of higher

critics. Their opinions on the book
would be chiefly useful as indicating
the limitations of their own faculties.

In like manner, the things, which
to the world seem real, were to the Christ
only shadows, while the things which
were real to Him were invisible to the
world. ' I stood,' He says in the beautiful saying attributed to Him in the
Logia, ' in the midst of the world and
in the flesh was I seen of them, and all
men found I drunken, and none found
I athirst among them, and my soul griev-
eth over the sons of men because they
are blind at heart.'

Perhaps it was inevitable that even
in the Christian Church the position of
the mystic should be most persistently
misunderstood. It is a mere matter
of history that the prevailing attitude
towards him on the part of the ecclesiastic has invariably been that of the
Prophet Balaam to his ass.

The conduct of the beast was to him

incomprehensible. She turned aside from his way, she thrust his foot against a wall, she fell down under him, *because she saw and he did not*. The mystic has always been more or less beaten with the rod of ecclesiastical authority. ' I would there were a sword in my hand, for now I would kill thee,' has often been the aspiration of Church conclaves. Yet Balaam was saved by his ass, as Christianity has been kept alive by mysticism.

It is obvious that it is only a minority who could truly say with the Apostle, ' We look not on the things which are seen, but on the things which are unseen,' and it is necessary in the economy of the Church that the majority who cannot, as yet, so look on the world and life should not be neglected. The distinction between them and the provision which should be made for both is strongly and repeatedly emphasized by our Lord.

' To you it is given to know the mysteries of the Kingdom of Heaven, but to them it is not given.'

' He that hath ears to hear let *him* hear.'

He provides for both classes ; knowledge of the mysteries for the developed few : parables for the undeveloped many. To both He reveals Himself according to their powers of seeing.

Man is like a house with two fronts. On one side of his being he faces the material world where all is perishable and transitory ; on the other side he looks out on the world which is real and spiritual and eternal. It is of course from the latter that he must ultimately welcome the real approach of the Christ. But just because in the earlier stage of his development his consciousness is centred on that side which looks out on the phenomenal world of shadows, because to him at first that alone seems real, because he cannot yet hear Him who on the other side of his being—far within—stands at the door and knocks, the Eternal Christ projects Himself into human history and approaches him by the pathway of the bodily senses, and so we have what we call the historic Incarnation.

It is useful in this connexion to recall Plato's wonderful allegory of the Cave. He imagines some men chained so that their faces were always turned towards the inner wall of the cave, and all they knew of the outer world was just what they saw of it in the shadows projected on that wall.

They themselves and all that they saw became identified in their minds with the shadows that they cast. The only world they knew was a world of two dimensions. To their stunted and impoverished minds it alone was real.

Then he imagines one of them escaping from his chains and learning to know the three-dimensional world in its reality and not only through its reflections on the wall. How could such a man if he rejoined his companions make clear to them the nature of the real world which he himself had come to know ?

That surely was just the problem of the Christ. Here was a world where the faces of men were turned fixedly towards the phenomenal and the unreal, and whose hearts were set on shadows. How could He bring them to turn and look the other way, to face the spiritual, to know the eternal and the true ?

He would approach them by the way of the senses. He would reveal Himself under conditions of time and space. He would project Himself into history. He would mingle with them in the shadow life of earth. He would win their confidence and love. He would tell them of the real world—His world—the Kingdom of God. He would speak to them of that He knew and testify of that He

had seen. He would seek to wean their
affections from earthly things and bid
His nearest followers sell all that they
had and follow Him homeless from place
to place till His Presence became the
one unchanging factor of their lives.
Then He would tell them of approaching
departure. He would say to them, ' A
little while and ye behold Me no more
(" with the wondering gaze of the bodily
senses ") and again a little while (when
the shock of the sense of loss is past—
when you have turned your faces towards
the world which is spiritual and real)
and then you shall *see* Me. Then you
shall never lose Me more. . . . And
now,' He would say, ' go back to your
fellow-men and do for them what I have
done for you. Hold before them my
historic life ; teach them to know Me
" after the flesh " ; tell them about My
world ; testify to them that " the things
which are seen are temporal, and the
things which are not seen are eternal."

Then they too will come to turn their backs on history—not repudiating it —not denying it—God forbid—why should they kick down the ladder by which they have climbed ?—but transcending it, till they too will be able to say, " If in the past we have known Christ after the flesh, yet now we know Him so no more." '

The historical bears a similar relation to the real that the map, say, of Scotland does to the country itself with its mountains and valleys, its fields, and its lochs. It is as true a representation as can be given on a piece of paper. It is accurate indeed but inadequate, suggestive not final. We must look beyond it to that which it represents. Knowledge of the land itself may enable us to transcend its use, but it will never justify us in repudiating its accuracy or denying its practical value. Nay, may we not say that it can only be through knowledge of the original that we can ultimately be able to verify the accuracy of the map ?

The Tabernacle which was the shadow of the heavenly things was glorious to every Hebrew but one, and that one was Moses, who had seen the heavenly realities of which it was but the dim reflection. None the less, and more than all the rest, Moses knew its value.

But it may be said, ' Does not this imply that the historic life of Christ is merely a parable ? ' To which we may answer, ' Yes, it is God's parable, and *God's parables are written in history.*'

It is necessary to emphasize this point in view of what has been written by some modernists and by exponents of ' The New Theology.' The Life of Christ is history, but it is not merely history and not mainly history. ' To them that are without,' indeed, it is history only, for ' to them all things are in parables,' but to those whose faces are turned to the eternal it is the manifestation to the eyes of men of what is going on all the time.

Perhaps no one has drawn this distinction more powerfully or more beautifully than Browning in the words which he puts into the mouth of the aged and dying St. John in the great poem, ' A Death in the Desert.'

'To me that story—ay, that Life and Death
  Of which I wrote "it was," to me, it is :
  — Is, here and now ! I apprehend nought else.
  Is not God now in the world His power first made ?
  Is not His love at issue still with sin,
  Visibly, when a wrong is done on earth ?
  Love, wrong, and pain, what see I else around !
  Yea, and the Resurrection and uprise
  To the right hand of the Throne—

    .   .   .   .   .

              —These are, I see :
  But ye, the children, His beloved ones too.
  Ye need—'

And then he describes an optic glass he once wondered at by means of which things ' lying confusedly insubordinate ' to the unassisted eye became at once distinct and small and clear.

'Just thus ye needs must apprehend what truth
I see, reduced to plain historic fact
Diminished into clearness proved a point
And far away : ye would withdraw your gaze
From out Eternity, strain it upon time,
Then stand before that fact, that Life and Death,
Stay there at gaze, till it dispart, dispread,
As though a star should open out, all sides,
Grow the world on you, as it is my world.'

The mystical deals with the real, the
timeless, the eternal ! The historical
is the reflection of the real under conditions of time and space.

Now the value of this postulate is
that it gives us a right in dealing with
the Gospel history to take an *à priori*
point of view. It makes intelligible
our definite refusal to treat the story of
the Life of Christ as mere ordinary history to be submitted unconditionally
to the dissection of critics with such
facts and faculties as they can bring
to bear upon it.

It has been truly said that ' Nothing
is less real than history.' Merely his-

torical events recede into the past and diminish in importance to us as the years go by. How far away, for intance, is the Boer War and the Battle of Colenso! 'What's Hecuba to him or he to Hecuba?' asks Hamlet. But the events of the Life of Christ never recede and never diminish in importance. And why? Because they are more than history. They are eternal truths made manifest in time.

You travel in a railway train by night. Houses flit by you and trees and villages. You see them for a moment and then they are lost in the darkness behind. But the moon flies face to face with you all the way. It is as near you at the end of your journey as at the beginning. Again we ask why?

Because it is lifted up out of the Earth's sphere. So with the Cross of Calvary, so with the Resurrection of the Christ. They are as near to us to-day as to our forefathers a thousand years ago : they will be as near to our descendants a thousand years hence as they are to us.

' I,' said Jesus, ' if I be lifted up out of the earth (ἐκ τῆς γῆς) will draw all men unto Me.'

The truths of which these events are the outward expression can be apprehended as really by the awakened intuitional faculty as the historical events themselves can be grasped by the human reason. Reason verifies what Faith sees, and common sense teaches us to approach the investigation rather to verify than to explore. Let us put this in the form of a fable.

An eagle and a mole once had an argument about what was happening a mile away. The eagle saw and bore witness; the mole travelled half a mile to investigate and died an unbeliever. The eagle having seen could not fail to have an *à priori* opinion about what the investigation would reveal. This was denounced by the mole as being quite contrary to all the canons of impartial research.

Thus we claim for mysticism that it gives us a renewed hold upon the facts of the Life of Christ.

' O foolish men,' says Jesus to the two disciples on the way to Emmaus, ' O foolish men and slow of heart to believe in all that the prophets have spoken! Behoved it not the Christ to suffer these things and to enter into His glory ? '

If they ought to have expected it before it happened it would seem to follow that something else beside historical criticism ought to have a say in the question whether it happened or not.

Reason is to Intuition what touch is to sight. We generally touch things with an *à priori* expectation at the back of our minds. Impartial investigation with the finger tips is a thing practically unknown. And yet how useful is the sense of touch !

'Is that a dagger that I see before me ?' says Macbeth.
  'The handle towards my hand, come let me clutch thee.
  I have thee not and yet I see thee still.'

The sense of touch frees us from taking up our time with 'daggers of the mind and false creations.'

Even such a help is the reason applied in criticism to the intuitions of faith. All the mystic claims is his right to see and to expect—the right—nay the duty of the Christian to adopt the standpoint enjoined by our Lord when He said, 'Behoved it not the Christ to suffer these things ?'

We grant at once the need of verification and the high utility of the critical sense. But verification is one thing and exploration is quite another. There is all the difference in the world between examining in the light and groping in the dark. Intuition is in most people an opening and as yet untrained sense, and without verification it is not to be absolutely relied on; but criticism without intuition, criticism which resolves to ignore the *à priori* point of view to which our Lord refers, *that* is hopeless blindness; and 'if the blind lead the blind,' where will they both end?

When the spiritual faculties of the most developed men—the poets and the prophets of our race—reach a certain level they begin to see the eternal truths in great flashes of intuition, flooding the soul with light. Then they look for that timeless truth to be reflected in time. They look backward into history, and if they do not see it there, then forward into the future in the spirit of prophecy.

If I drop a coin on the floor I do not look to see *if* it is there. I know it is there and look to find it.

But it may be said, 'That theory is all very well for those with mystical insight,

16

but what about the majority ? ' Well,
let us frankly recognize the distinction
and provide for both. That again is
Bible teaching, though strangely ignored.

' We speak wisdom,' says St. Paul,
' among them that are perfect.' But
he provides for the others too. He feeds
the ' babes in Christ ' with milk.

That surely is the real significance of
the distinction made by the risen Christ
to St. Peter, ' Feed My lambs '—' Feed
My sheep.'

His standard of maturity was not a
physical one.

Let us spend less time in trying to
convince the reason of that which transcends it and spend more in developing
the spiritual faculty by which alone it
can be apprehended.

' Spiritual things are spiritually dis-
cerned.' ' If any man will do His will,
he shall know of the doctrine.'

It is not faultless syllogisms that we
need, but awakened faculties. We have

no quarrel with Biblical criticism, though we may sometimes feel that the primal curse on the serpent lies somewhat heavily on those critics who, while possessing scholarship, lack insight.

If we may go back for a moment to what was said a little ago that reason with all its machinery of criticism and investigation is to intuition what touch is to sight, it will be plain that while we give pre-eminence to the latter we readily acknowledge the value of both.   What we utterly condemn is the tacit assumption of some critics that our faith in historic Christianity depends on what they can find out from their old manuscripts.

It would be equally reasonable to claim that since optical illusions are possible all our knowledge of this world must be acquired through the finger tips.

Biblical criticism may brandish its results and its theories in the face of the ecclesiastic and frighten him out of his wits, but for the mystic it has no terrors.

The Anchor of his faith has never been grappled to merely external testimony, but—to use the great mixed metaphor of the writer of the Epistle to the Hebrews—' entereth into that which is within the veil' and beyond the senses and the reasoning of men.

Now if the events of the Life of Christ are the reflection in time and space of great Eternal truths, then we can understand His own calm certainty that His every step was in the path marked out for Him, why He seemed to move according to a chart along an inevitable path, and why these events correspond with and appeal to the spiritual experience of the spiritual man in every age. In this spiritual correspondence we find the ultimate basis of belief.

The eternal truth that ' Jesus Christ cometh (keeps on coming) in the flesh' is narrowed down through the ' optic glass' of history to the Birth in Bethlehem, and finds its counterpart in the individual life of man when, in the words of St. Paul, ' The Christ is formed ' in him. The age-long struggle of love with sin is expressed and manifested in the Cross of Calvary and reproduced in the individual experience of those who are ' crucified with Christ.'

And so we might watch Him pass from His Passion to the Resurrection ' power of an endless life '—to His Ascension or withdrawal from the physical that He might fill (or inter-penetrate) all things and so come nearer to all, and then think of Him as no longer chained to form, no longer ex-ternal to us, but seeking entrance from within and manifesting Himself to us, and in us, and through us.

Thus the Life of Christ becomes clothed to us with new and living power. It is no longer mere ancient history, but the revelation of present and eternal truth.

> ' And warm, sweet, tender, even yet
> A present help is He
> And Faith has still its Olivet
> And Love its Galilee.'

History and Mysticism

X

History and Mysticism

LORD LEIGHTON used to tell how once when he was painting one of his autumn pictures in the Scottish Highlands a countryman came beside him and looked on in silence for a while. At last he spoke. 'Man,' he said, 'did ye never try photography ? '

'No,' said Lord Leighton, 'I can't say I have ever tried it.'

'It's a hantle quicker,' said the man, and then as a parting shot he added, 'And it's mair like the place.'

The story may serve to illustrate the contrast between the standpoints of the photographer and the painter, the mathematician and the poet, and what

is more important for the subject of
this chapter, it illustrates two different
ways of regarding history. Is it the
function of the true historian merely
to register facts as a photograph registers
the position of leaves and branches at
a particular moment, or is he to be
allowed the freedom of the painter to
depict what no photograph can reflect
but what the inner eye can see ? Are
the highest ends of truth better served
by the methods of the photographer or
by the methods of the painter ?

Let us take an illustration. The great
painters often represent the Infant
Christ with His little hand raised in
benediction. Would a photograph—if
there had been photographs in those
days—ever have obtained such a result ?
Yet would any realistic picture of a
Jewish infant ' taken from life ' express
with anything like the same truthfulness
the purpose and meaning of the incarnate
life ?

Or again, think of Raphael's great picture of the Transfiguration, in which with true prophetic insight he blends in one canvas the scene of wonder and heavenly stillness and beauty upon the Holy Mount with the anxiety, distraction and misery of the scene below. No photograph could have produced that result, but the painter was great enough to know when to sacrifice realism to reality, and history to truth.

The contrast between the standpoint of Lord Leighton and that of his rustic critic is seen again in the comparison of the pictures of the Nativity by the great Italian Masters with the treatment of the same subject in some modern realistic pictures.

These latter are based on the Scottish countryman's conception of reality. The painter gets some young Jewish mother to sit for his picture and paints just what any ordinary eye can see. He produces a result 'mair like the

place ' than the earlier painters achieve.
In their pictures the Heaven world is
breaking through, Angel wings are hov-
ering above, and the transitory world
is seen for a moment in the glow of that
' light that never was on sea or land.'

But which pictures reveal most fully
the truth of what really took place ?
And what are prophets for unless to
reveal with their higher faculties that
which the ordinary man with his lower
faculties would *not* see ?

I have more than once tried to get
an artist to paint a picture of what a
man would look like as seen by a mole,
but I have failed, as the artist seemed—
quite wrongly—to discern in the request
not a compliment to his power of imagination but some sinister personal reflection on his powers of vision. It is
not difficult, however, to conceive what
it might be like. A portion of a pair
of boots shading into mist and darkness
and far distances would represent the

similitude of 'the beauty of the world, the paragon of animals.' Certainly it would not be like a man as we know him, but the mole would have as much right as the realist to maintain that that picture represented what was actually there apart from 'fanciful nonsense.' We might even let our imagination take a higher flight and wonder what a man would be like as seen by an Angel. He would be visible, we should fancy, not so much in the lines and curves and colours of face and figure as in the nature, quality and intensity of his desires and thoughts. Any one who compares Doré's coarse pictures of the Paolo and Francesca of Dante's Vision driven before the storm blasts of Hell with the noble painting of the same subject by G. F. Watts will recognize the different points of view referred to.

The realist fancies that he is limiting his picture to what is there. As a matter

of fact he is only revealing how little
he can see. His realism and that of
the mole differ only in degree.

Now is it not possible to imagine that
the great prophet-historians of the
Hebrew race have treated history much
as Raphael treated the story of the
Transfiguration and as the Italian Masters treated the Nativity ? They have
helped history to give birth to truth.
For history is the reflection of the
eternal in the transitory. It is truth
striving, in spite of difficulties, to express
itself in action. It is the medium in
which God's parables are written. Yes,
but the medium is inadequate for its
work—as inadequate to be the vehicle
of truth as the length and breadth of a
picture canvas to express the three-
dimensional events which it portrays.
Line and curve, light and shadow, have
to be brought in to help the deficiency
and to suggest to the imagination what
cannot be depicted, and thus all the

painter's art contributes to the expression of truth.

In a similar way history from, let us say, an Angel's point of view is a useful but quite inadequate medium for the working out of God's parables, for the reflection under conditions of time and space of His eternal truths.

Our consciousness is centred in a world where—if we could only realize it—all is shadow and where nothing lasts. We are like children looking at trees reflected in the still waters of a lake. So clear they seem that we can scarcely help asking, Can you deny their reality ? A storm comes and we almost wonder, Did they ever exist ? Then we look up to the trees which threw the reflection and *they* remain in storm and sunshine alike. Even so the things of creation, as Plato taught us long ago, are just the projection of God's thoughts upon the ever-changing ocean of matter. They are reflections in three dimensions indeed, but not less reflections for that. They form and break; they arise from and return to the ocean of matter. The real permanency is not in the reflections but in that which they reflect.

The value of art is not in the finite things which it portrays, but in the infinite which it suggests. That at least would be the opinion of the painter, though not of the man who preferred photography.

Similarly, are we not right in saying that the purpose of history is not so much to register facts as to reveal truth? Its value is that in it are reflected the purposes and the parables of God, and God's parables are written in history.

Of course one anticipates the obvious objection that this theory of the true function of the historian would seem to justify every enthusiast in writing history 'to order' so to speak. But history, like painting, is an art, and real

history can only be written by great
seers just as real paintings can only be
produced by great artists. Any school-
boy can mess a canvas with oil paints
and call it a picture, as any enthusiast
can distort facts and call it history,
but such ' pictures ' and such ' history '
soon sink into the obscurity which their
merits demand.

We may say that the drama is to
history what history is to truth. The
drama reflects history vividly but in-
adequately, and with obvious and inevitable limitations. It crowds a lifetime
into an hour, but it reveals the salient
points of the life. It needs amplifica-
tion and supplementing if it is to represent history.

Now let us imagine a race of people
who only know history as it is represented
in the drama. The stage is their world.
Its events are to them the only realities,
and they are quite unconscious of its
limitations. Let us suppose that they

17

are familiar with the play of *Richard III*, and know intimately every scene and every saying. Then a professor of history appears who knows the life as it took place, and lectures to them on the subject. He has to supplement the stage account, to fill in its bald outlines, to round off with the story of years its abrupt transitions, to modify some vivid scene, to expand here, to contract there, to supply what is lacking somewhere else.

At once protests arise. The professor is destroying their world. He tells them that theirs is not the real world but only its reflection. His own account is the true record. Then why, they ask, was it not so reflected? Because of the nature of the case, he answers, because of the limitations of the drama as a reflector.

Now every argument that the historian can use against the imagined people of the stage-world, the mystic can use to the realistic historian and the painter to the believer in photography.

' All the world's a stage,' as Jacques says, and history, like the drama and like photography, tells all it can. Prophets and seers, poets and painters exist in order to fill in their imperfections.

Now this is just what we seem to catch St. Paul—or rather the unknown author of the Jewish tradition he was quoting—in the very act of doing. He tells us that the things which happened to the Hebrews in their exodus ' happened unto them by way of example,' and he amplifies the Mosaic account by stating that ' they drank of a spiritual rock that followed them: and the rock was Christ.'

The great Apostle seems here to be assisting history in the interests of truth. To one who regards the Bible as the inspired revelation to men of the realities of the spiritual world, it could not seem an extravagant thought that the great

unseen Beings who under God direct
and control the progress of the world—
the true 'Kings of the Earth'—use
history as far as it can be used to work
out in parable His great age-long truths.

How important, for example, that
men should have before them vividly
and in concrete form the tremendous
age-long drama of the deliverance of
humanity from the sordid bondage of
materialism into the glorious liberty
of its true home in the spiritual world!
In order that this parable might be
written in history we see a race most
carefully selected, separated and prepared. It is driven into Egypt by
famine and suffers bondage until its
great prophet and leader arises, and
then follow its deliverance, guidance
and sustenance in the wilderness, its
battles, failures, and triumphs, until at
length the Jordan is crossed and the
promised land attained.

What the exact incidents of that

exodus were as they might have appeared to a Scottish photographer or
been described by a modern newspaper
correspondent, seems perhaps to be a
matter of secondary importance. The
great Hebrew prophet-historians saw the
realities of which the events in the
physical world were the inadequate
reflection. Again and again both in
the Old Testament and in the New
the world-wide, age-long significance of
Hebrew history was strongly emphasized.
'These things happened unto them by
way of example' and 'They were
written for our admonition.' The grand
description of the guidance of the host
by the pillar of cloud by day and of fire
by night is in the deepest sense a statement of real truth. Whether or not
that cloud would have made any im-
pression on the film of a modern camera
we do not know and we need not care.
God's purposes and man's spiritual history were wonderfully made manifest

and carefully worked out in the history of this selected race in so far as history could lend itself to the purpose; but where history breaks down the vision of the seer comes to its aid. The truth with which St. Paul was concerned in the passage quoted above was the deliverance of men from 'the bondage of corruption' and mortality into the promised land of the spiritual life. He dealt with the fact rather than the reflection, and he assisted the reflection to give expression to the fact.

It is surely at least as difficult to work out this theme in history as it would be for us to translate *Paradise Lost* into the language of the Australian aborigines. No doubt it could be done, but how terribly the sublimity, the glory, and the mystery would be stripped from it by the limitations of that miserable vocabulary! How the translator would long to call in the aid of art to amplify by line and colour the poverty-stricken reflection of mighty thoughts and scenes ! How he would sympathize with St. Paul's bold endeavour to bring Hebrew history into still closer approximation to revealed truth ! Historical ' facts ' are the lines and pigments of the Divine Artist, and are meant less to register what is seen by the bodily eye than to suggest the great spiritual realities which are invisible to it. The prophet will not be confined to what the world calls ' facts.' He spends his life in trying to break through them and get behind them.

' To find their meaning is his meat and drink.'

Now it is just here that the remarkable revival of Mysticism in our own times is coming to our aid. It does not quarrel with ' facts,' but it puts them in their right place. It raises no protest against the ascertained results of Higher Criticism, though it smilingly points out that many critics take themselves far too seriously. It insists that men should come to a clear understanding as to what is meant by reality. To most men the transitory is the real world, and hence its events and facts assume an absurdly exaggerated importance. To the mystic, on the other hand, the real world is the spiritual, and nothing that happens under conditions of time and space can be anything but reflections. For example, he would not say that the salvation of the world depended on what happened on Calvary, but that what happened on Calvary made manifest once for all the eternal Sacrifice on which the salvation of the world depends. He does not think of the Virgin Birth at Bethlehem as the coming of the eternal Word into the world, but as the manifestation to the world that He is there all the time. That surely is the lifting up of the Son of Man 'out of the earth' which will draw all men unto Him.

The Seven Trumpets

XI

The Seven Trumpets

THE Seven Trumpets, and—in a
terrible crescendo—the Seven
Bowls are a revelation of the Divine
resources in meeting and punishing and
overthrowing opposition to the purposes
of God. The persecuted Church, weak and
poor and scattered, kept saying, amid
its bitter sufferings, "Thine is the
Power," and the unveiling of what God
could do was as grateful as it was necessary. The vision of the angels with
the Seven Trumpets emerges during the
silence which follows the loosing of the
Seventh Seal. Their trumpets of doom
are given to them and they stand ready
to act, but in a striking figure it is revealed that these shattering forces by
which the power of evil on earth is to be

broken await the prayers of the saints.
An angel stands at the Altar to present
before God these prayers mingled with
the incense which he offers.   Then he
fills with fire from the Altar the censer
he has been using and casts it upon the
earth, and there follow voices and thun-
derings and lightnings and an earthquake.   So closely is the power of God
associated with the prayer of man.

Here, as in the other sets of seven, the
series is broken up into two parts, con-
taining respectively the numbers four
and three, and here, as in the other cases,
the basis of the division is the same.   The
first four trumpets herald judgments on
the earth, the sea, the rivers and fountains of water, and on the heavens.   We
have seen that in Apocalyptic language
the earth is taken to represent the physical world, the waters to represent the
world of emotion and desires, while
the mental world is represented by the
heavens.   It is to be noted, however,

here and in the case of the Seven Bowls,
the vision divides the waters into two
kinds, the sea, and the rivers and fountains of waters.   Perhaps the distinction
may refer to the sea on the one hand
as the general emotional element, and on
the other to the sources and springs of
desire in the world of thought.   In any
case it enables the sevenfold structure
to be completed in the normal way.
Thus the first four Trumpets deal with
the whole range of temporal judgments,
while the last three " Woes " are definitely spiritual in their character.   This
division of the seven into four, which deal
with temporal judgments, and three with
spiritual, is just what, by analogy, the
student of the Apocalypse has the right
to expect.   Yet, strangely enough, the
fact that the first four trumpets deal
with what is temporal appears to Dr.
Charles strong evidence that they should
not be in the text at all.   With their
" colourless cosmic visitations " they

" arrest," he says, " the natural development of the book." I should not myself think it easy to find a more unsuitable word than " colourless " to describe the vision of the burning mountain cast into the reddening sea, or of the great star called wormwood, " burning as a torch," falling upon the rivers and upon the fountains of waters. But having decided in his own mind that the heptadic structure of this vision of the Trumpets is altogether wrong, Dr. Charles proceeds to break down the carved work thereof with axes and hammers. Verse viii. 2, which, by its position, teaches the beautiful lesson that the putting forth of Divine power waits on—and is closely connected with—the prayers of the saints, is abandoned as an intrusion in its present position, and any words which suggest the larger number are simply struck out as interpolations. A more unhappy method of dealing with the text of Scripture it would be hard to find. The

chapter stands, after Dr. Charles has done
with it, like the carved work in Wor-
cester Cathedral, after the puritan visitation ; or, perhaps, in view of the excel-
lence of his intentions, it would be fairer
to say, like an ancient Gothic church
after a mid-Victorian " restoration."

To return to the text as we have it,
unrestored and complete, we notice that
each of the judgments of the first four
trumpets affects one-third of that on
which it falls. The figure of course is
in no sense literal, but it indicates a
calamity limited indeed, but of terrible
severity, affecting the physical, emotional,
and mental faculties of men.

Just as the loosing of the fifth Seal
brought before us a region beyond the
reach of the physical consciousness, so
the sounding of the fifth Trumpet heralds
a judgment which is distinctly spiritual
in its nature and pierces deeper than even
to the affections and thoughts—" And
the fifth angel sounded and I saw a

star fallen from heaven to the earth."

It is impossible not to associate these words with the saying of our Lord in St. Luke x. 18, "I beheld Satan as lightning fallen from heaven." We may take it that the fallen star refers to the master power among "the world-rulers of this darkness," the organizing spirit of evil in "the heavenly places" or world of intellect. To him is given "the key of the abyss" and authority to draw on its dread resources in his efforts to injure man in his spiritual nature. Power is given to him, but alike in the time and scope of its exercise it is strictly limited. "The key of the abyss" is a remarkable phrase, and at least it indicates that this kind of assault is one from which in ordinary circumstances men are exempt. It reveals, too, that moral degradation and corruption of the will is the most appalling punishment for deliberate and persistent sin. As the pit is opened demonic beings like a thick cloud of smoke arise from it, darkening the air and veiling the sun. The meaning seems to be that the intellect is terribly darkened by the perverted will. The seer exhausts the power of language in describing the savage, subtle, and cruel nature of these demons, the whole being of those whom they attack is poisoned and tortured as with the stroke of a scorpion; yet their power can only be exercised against those who have not the seal of God in their foreheads.

With the sounding of the Sixth Trumpet begins the second "Woe." A voice is heard from the four horns of the golden Altar before God saying, "Loose the four angels which were bound at the great river Euphrates." The voice from the four horns of the golden altar tells us two things: first, that the coming Woe is to be world-wide in its scope; and next, that the impending judgment is closely connected with human prayer. But what are we to understand by the

18

four angels ? They are plainly angels
of destruction, their mission is to slay.
They are to carry out a judgment which
has been long waiting and which has
been fixed for an exact and definite time.
But why are they bound at the river
Euphrates ? I think we have the solution if we connect the passage with the
tremendous curse pronounced upon Babylon in the 50th and 51st chapters of
Jeremiah. The prophet instructed Se-
raiah to read the curse and then to tie
a stone to the writing and cast it into the
Euphrates, saying, "Thus shall Babylon
sink and not rise from the evil which I
will bring upon her."

It is altogether in keeping with the
character of this book to see in the perse-
cuting power of Babylon and in its
destruction the type of the hostile world-
power which had long held the people of
God in captivity and whose doom is
now definitely fixed. Just as the historic
Israel is in the Apocalypse merged in

redeemed humanity in all the completeness of the 144,000 dwelling in heavenly
light, so Babylon, the old historic oppressor, becomes ultimately identified
with the power of the world in its age-
long struggle with the Church of God,
and the scope of the curse of Jeremiah—
the Babylonian woe—correspondingly
expands.

It is interesting to recall that at the
opening of the Sixth Seal four angels
were revealed standing at the four corners
of the earth ready to let loose the four
destroying winds ; at the sounding of
the Sixth Trumpet in like manner four
angels are shown ready from a particular
point to go forth on their destroying work.
The four-fold direction of these destructive agents indicates the universal character of the world-power with which the
Church has waged its long fight.

www.ingramcontent.com/pod-product-compliance
Lightning Source LLC
Chambersburg PA
CBHW060309100426
42812CB00003B/710